50 WAYS TO LIVEN UP YOUR MEETINGS

50 Ways to Liven Up Your Meetings

GRAHAM ROBERTS-PHELPS

Gower

Published by
Gower Publishing Limited
Gower House
Croft Road
Aldershot
Hampshire GU11 3HR
England

Gower Publishing Company
131 Main Street
Burlington VT 05401–5600 USA

Graham Roberts-Phelps has asserted his right under the Copyright, Designs and Patents Act 1988 to be identified as the author of this work.

British Library Cataloguing in Publication Data
Roberts-Phelps, Graham
  50 ways to liven up your meetings
  1. Business meetings
  I. Title II. Fifty ways to liven up your meetings
  658.4'56

ISBN 0–566–08392–2

Library of Congress Cataloging-in-Publication Data
Roberts-Phelps, Graham.
  50 ways to liven up your meetings/Graham Roberts-Phelps.
    p. cm.
  ISBN 0–566–08392–2 (hardback)
  1. Business meetings. I. Title: 50 ways to liven up your meetings.
II. Title.
HF5734.5.R63 2000
658.4'56–dc21   00–042974

Typeset in 11 point Palatino by Bournemouth Colour Press, Parkstone and printed in Great Britain by MPG Books Limited, Bodmin.

Contents

Introduction

50 Ways to Liven Up Your Meetings is a collection of, ice-breaking, energizing *and* meeting-boosting games, activities and exercises for use in almost any kind of meeting – for example:

- Regular team meetings
- Board meetings
- Informal discussions
- Customer meetings
- Department meetings and briefings
- Management reviews.

Each activity is designed to make your meeting more effective, interactive and engaging.

Designed and collated by Graham Roberts-Phelps, each idea has been carefully tried and tested in a number of different meeting environments. The effect of using the right activity at the right time will help achieve one or more of the following aims:

- Increase participation
- Stimulate creativity
- Increase rapport and understanding
- Generate more ideas and discussion
- Start or end a session with a 'buzz'
- Reduce boredom – keep more people awake
- Have fun.

If you have any suggestions for inclusion in a future volume, or have any questions regarding these activities please contact 80/20 Training Ltd on (44) 01908 587462.

Six tips to get the best out of this book

1. Use the techniques with confidence

> All the ideas in this book have been developed and used in professional meetings and seminars, and are all proven to be effective for a number of different applications.

2. Be flexible

> Because of the 'open content' style, they are suitable for most types of organization and meeting. This approach also makes them easy to adapt, or tailor, to fit your needs and organization. Don't hesitate to vary the exercises, adding in new elements or expanding various segments. You will also find that the exercises will vary in their execution, as different groups of people will tackle the same exercise in different ways.

3. Structure your meeting

> By mixing at least three different formats (working in small groups/pairs, as individuals and as a whole group) to cover the same points, you can greatly increase learning retention and effectiveness. Also, vary the balance between working in small groups, the group as a whole and individual work. People will have different preferences and gain more from a variety of formats during a meeting.

4. Make notes and adapt

> Customize or edit these ways or ideas to better suit your own style of meeting as you gain experience in running them. Make notes in the margin, either whilst preparing or during a meeting in order to remember the points for next time.

5. Facilitate, don't dominate

> These techniques are designed to help people work together and interact. If you find yourself talking rather less than you might do normally, don't worry about it!

6. Prepare yourself fully

> As a general rule of thumb you should spend at least twice as much time preparing to use any technique as it will actually take

to run. Think about the questions you should ask and the questions others will ask of you.

Types of working when using the '50 Ways'

Individual working

When participants are required to work on their own, perhaps completing a questionnaire or worksheet, it allows for a degree of self-reflection and is an excellent contrast to group work. Many people are happy working in this way; indeed, it follows the pattern of learning established at school.

Pairs

Based on the principle that 'two heads are better that one', this format needs participants to work in pairs, working through a problem, questionnaire or worksheet jointly.

It is often useful to pair people carefully, balancing personalities and experience. Make sure that both are contributing and making notes. In longer meetings it is a good idea to change these pairs occasionally. If you have an odd number of participants, stretch one group to three.

Small groups

Small group of 3–8 people are most suitable for working on a problem, issue or discussion, as well as in free-format ideas sessions.

The size of your main group will, of course, determine how small you can divide the groups, but from general observation it is difficult to circulate between, or monitor, more than about four groups.

Main group discussion

In this format you may run a general discussion or activity with the whole group of eight or more people.

Part I

Ideas to improve your management of meetings

Managing meetings

Effective, efficient and enjoyable

Badly managed meetings can waste an enormous number of working hours, simply because more than one person's time can be wasted simultaneously! You can make your meetings much more cost-effective by making sure they are as effective, efficient and enjoyable as possible.

- **Effective.** Did the meeting achieve its purpose or intended outcome?
- **Efficient.** How well was time managed?
- **Enjoyable.** Did you and others find it a positive or useful experience? Would you look forward to the next one?

Some hints on leading effective meetings

1. Each agenda item should be phrased as a question, requiring a decision to be made on how best to achieve a clear objective.
2. The agenda should be arranged in order of the importance of the decisions to be made.
3. The tenor of the meeting must be very clearly to decide what is right and not who is right; personal pride and status must be set aside in the cause of making the best decision.
4. The minutes of the meeting should be built around clear statements of who should do what and by when.
5. All decisions made must be followed up to ensure that the agreed actions are taken.
6. Don't feel obliged to involve everyone for the entire meeting if they are only concerned with some of the content; adjust the order of the agenda to group together

the issues that concern particular individuals.

7. As a meeting leader maintain a firm but subtle control, but remain sensitive to the feelings of individuals and be prepared to be flexible about the agenda if necessary.

8. Everyone must be given an equal opportunity to state their views without feeling pressured into a contribution.

9. Make time to listen to what *everyone* is saying (or trying to say); the poor communicator may have an excellent idea and the really obstinate person who annoys everyone else often has some good basic points to make.

10. Ensure that the meeting is paced properly in terms of breaks, changes of pace, type of activity or topic and so on. Using ice-breakers and energizers can help keep people alert and 'awake'.

Running meetings

The following checklist covers the stages for planning and running effective meetings:

1. Set the aims.
2. Prepare the information.
3. Plan how the meeting will be run.
4. Run the meeting.
5. Review and learn.

Set the aims

- What is the meeting for?
- What must you have achieved by the end of the meeting?
- What actions should result from the meeting?

If you are unable to answer these questions, do not call a meeting. If you go ahead, make sure that the aims are realistic.

Prepare the information

- What do *you* know already, and what else do you need to find out beforehand, about the subject and the members of the meeting?
- What do the members need to know in advance and how should they prepare?

Plan how the meeting will be run

Make sure that you spend at least some time considering the following:

- **Facilities:**
  - Where will you hold the meeting?
  - What handouts are needed?
  - What do you need in the way of audiovisual or other equipment?
- **Structure/agenda:**
  - What is the priority (and consequently the sequence of) agenda items?
  - How long have you allowed for each?
- **Preparation:**
  - Are you (and the group) clear about the aims of the meeting?
  - What information should you give out at the start of the meeting?
  - What will be the 'rules' of the meeting – the process to which the group will adhere?

Run the meeting

Try to lead by example with the following key behaviours:

- Proposing ideas, solutions and plans.
- Building and supporting the ideas of others.
- Testing understanding to make sure that your conclusions are clear and shared by all. (Play the role of devil's advocate if necessary.)
- Summarizing your conclusions, agreements and action points.

After the meeting review and learn:

- Did you achieve your aims? If so, why? If not, why not? Did the problem lie in the aims, preparation, plan or behaviour?
- What improvements can you plan for future meetings?
- How did everyone taking part feel about the meeting and their role within it?

Setting aims

What are aims for?

It is vital to think through the aims of a meeting as extensively and as precisely as you can because they determine all other requirements. Also, purposeful aims must be set for meetings in order to:

- Decide what information you need to prepare before you can even plan the meeting, thus avoiding wasted time during the meeting.
- Work out a plan of how you propose to run the meeting. You must have aims in order to know how to lead the discussion.
- Keep to your plan when running the meeting. Aimless, unplanned meetings collapse into conflict or indifference.
- After the meeting review to determine whether the meeting was successful, and what you can learn from it in order to improve your future meetings.

Aims must be purposes, not merely reasons

First, decide what each meeting is for – what results must be achieved. There is an important difference between purposes and reasons:

- **Purposes** are determined by asking the question 'What is this meeting for?' and starting the answer with 'In order to achieve ...?'.
- **Reasons** why the meeting is being held are determined by asking the question 'Why am I holding the meeting?' This does not give you the purpose as you will only get an answer which begins with 'Because ...' – for example, 'Because we always have a meeting at this time in the month'.

Make the aims realistic

As well as being purposeful, aims must also be realistic. The following questions will help you decide whether or not they are.

- Is the issue resolvable? A meeting is not a remedy. It cannot work miracles and put right problems which exist for reasons quite different from the lack of a meeting!

11

- Can the people who you have in mind to attend achieve the aims? Do they know enough? Do they care enough? Do they have enough authority?
- Can the aims be achieved in the time available? You cannot say 'Sorry I had to rush through the second half of the agenda, and there just wasn't time', as if it was not your fault.

There are two points to remember: 'the aims' and 'the time'. Look at the relationship between these two pessimistically. Meetings usually take longer than you expect.

Ask yourself whether 'the aims' can be achieved 'in the time' available. If not, either make more time or reduce the aims to what can be achieved in the time available.

There can be no excuses – you should always have control over at least one of these two elements.

Preparing information

You should know already, or find out before planning, the following information.

The problem

If the purpose of the meeting is to resolve a problem, what is the definition of that problem and why does it exist? Define the causes, not just the symptoms.

The context

- Is the meeting one of a series about a sequence of events? (For example, launch planning.)
- What is the sequence of events and where are you up to so far?
- Is the meeting about one particular aspect of a wider issue? (For example, labour costs as part of a total cost problem.)
- What is the background history or politics?
- What past experience is available on similar or parallel cases?
- What relevant reports should be available?
- What are the relevant points from other meetings?

Up-to-date facts and figures

A meeting is not the best arena for sorting out complex and detailed data. The more you organize data before the meeting, the less danger there is of conflict through uninformed opinions. Accurate and current information on budgets and resources is important for many meetings.

- Who will prepare convincing facts and figures?

Definition of terms

A frequent problem with meetings, particularly about something initially abstract, such as 'communications' is that the issue is not defined, so that everybody talks about something different.

Supporting evidence, illustrations and examples

The purpose of supporting evidence, illustrations and examples is to capture and keep the interest of members, guide them into objective discussions and convince them.

Meeting planner

The following meeting planner is designed to help you structure your preparation for a meeting.

Meeting planner

Purpose of meeting:

Decisions to be reached:
1.
2.
3.

Attendees	Contribution

Does everybody above really need to attend   Yes   No

AGENDA (Prioritize and add timings for each point)

1.

2.

3.

4.

5.

Date:	Start time: End time:

Location:

Things to prepare/check

Meeting presentation tips

Meetings are often used as a means of conveying information, usually in the form of presentations, which can be subsequently discussed.

Most people dread or, at the very least, do not enjoy giving presentations. Many more people have experienced overlong and dull presentations. The following ideas might help with both aspects.

How information is absorbed within a presentation

The following points are important for the recall of information:

- People tend to remember most effectively information that is presented at the beginning and the end of a session. Material in the middle, particularly in a long presentation, can easily be lost.
- The longer a presentation lasts, the less benefit additional information has; the audience's concentration begins to wander and distractions creep in. More importantly, people commit facts to memory by organizing them into a structure in the mind, often unconsciously, during a period when the mind is not concentrating on the subject at hand. In a long presentation, people's minds become saturated with facts, which they have not had an opportunity to fit into any framework. Unstructured facts may displace other unstructured facts, resulting in confusion.
- Information that is effectively related to other information within the presentation – whether by showing linkages, fitting into a structure or repetition – is better remembered

than information that stands alone.

- Recall of material is often greatest not during a period of instructions but ten minutes after a presentation has finished: by then, the audience will have had time to fit information into appropriate mental structures. After this, recall of facts declines rapidly, so that, after a number of months, only a tiny percentage of the information covered may be remembered, *unless* information is regularly reviewed.
- Even very quick reviews of information can be extremely effective in the presentation of a topic, as they keep the overall framework, into which information is to be fitted, fresh and alive.
- Information is most effectively remembered when the whole mind is engaged in a presentation, not just the eyes or ears alone. Complex ideas are often easier to think about and convey if they are linked to familiar ones. An easily remembered, or visualized structure aids recall.

Designing a presentation for maximum retention and participation

These observations, and the manner in which information is assimilated, allow us to derive a number of principles by which presentations, lessons and meeting programmes can be delivered to have the maximum impact:

- Use breaks effectively – by breaking frequently, you take advantage of the way in which the mind recalls information most effectively at the beginning and end of a presentation. You can take advantage of this several times within a session, before and after each break.
- As a guide, presentations of less than 15–20 minutes in length can be ineffective, as it can be difficult for the audience to grasp the shape and rhythm of the material. Presentations of more than 50 minutes in length are usually boring and ineffective.
- Take advantage of the high initial level of assimilation and of the heightened understanding of the final facts to present some of the most important information during these periods.
- Relate facts that should be remembered to other facts and fit them into a framework that shows their relevance. If necessary, repeat important information.

- If the presentation is part of a series, spend a short time before the start reviewing the overall structure of previous presentations. This helps refresh the audience's minds with the information on which you want to build and allows connections to be made automatically which would otherwise be lost.
- Where possible, encourage members of the audience to review information in their own time.
- Try to engage the whole minds of your audience, and as many of their senses as practicable, with a variety of aids. This will keep them focused on the learning experience instead of letting unused parts of their minds 'wander off' and generate distractions.
- If possible, try to fit the key information to be recalled into a mnemonic structure. However, make sure that your audience understands and is comfortable with the use of memory techniques – otherwise your presentations may seem a little strange!
- Design the structure of a presentation to fit in with the way in which your audience recalls and assimilates information. This involves reviewing information already known, keeping presentations relatively short while still maintaining the feeling of structure, and presenting or re-presenting key information at the beginning and end of a session.

You may find the Presentation Preparation Worksheet on page 21 helpful when designing and planning your presentation.

Communicating with a group

Presenting to a small group can often be just as intimidating as presenting to a large group. Although there is much to learn about presentation skills, it can be made considerably easier by following a few key guidelines:

- Know your objective, and stick to it.
- Act confidently and be seen to believe in what you are saying.
- Be enthusiastic where appropriate.
- Be attentive to the audience's response and reactions (read body language).
- Prepare. Prepare. Prepare.
- Know your subject; it will give you confidence and build conviction in your audience.

- Know your audience; view things from their perspective and relate constantly to their own situation.
- KISS – Keep It Simple and Short – or, as Winston Churchill once said, 'Be precise, be brief, and be seated'.
- Check for understanding by asking questions and seeking positive confirmation that key points are understood.
- Use quotes, examples, references, stories, case studies, graphs – anything to bring the presentation to life.
- Paint vivid word pictures – use the language of an artful storyteller with vivid verbs and active adjectives.
- Vary your voice tone – emphasize words and sentences by lowering or raising your voice. Also vary the pitch, speed, tone and pace to maintain attention and keep interest.

Using audio-visual aids

Overhead projector (OHP)

The overhead projector is undoubtedly a valuable resource for meeting organizers or presenters. It allows the use of pre-prepared visual material and can serve to increase learning retention and maintain interest. Here are a few key guidelines to making best use of an OHP:

- Make sure everyone can see it. (This may not always be as easy as it sounds, as often the projector itself may be in the way. If this is the case, place it on a small low table.)
- Test the projector before you start, including a spare bulb. Make sure that it is focused, ready for the first slide.
- Use bold text, and colours if possible. Don't make slides too 'busy'.
- Use frames and number your slides. As you use them, keep them in order in case you need to refer back to an earlier slide.
- Write notes in the frame margins to help you, or use Post-its to make notes.
- Turn the projector off in between slides. Not only is the slide distracting, but so is the noise.
- Keep messages and key points on the slides short. Sentences should be no longer than 15 words.
- 'Reveal' slides, one point at a time, using a piece of card (paper tends to fall off). If you are changing slides quickly, leave the OHP running.
- Make good use of graphs, diagrams and pictures.

Flipchart

The trusty flipchart is often the mainstay of a meeting programme in that it can allow for both preprepared visuals and spontaneous note-taking. It can also maintain interest and help emphasize key points. Guidelines for use are as follows:

- Use the flipchart to help keep a presentation interesting, adding, as it does, action and movement.
- Check that you have enough paper and pens (that work) before you start.
- Use big bold words and writing that is clear to read.
- Use the flipchart to summarize and make notes, graphs or charts (especially useful when spontaneous).
- Occasionally ask one of the participants to do the writing to maintain participant involvement.
- Don't talk to the flipchart, except when reviewing what has been written down.
- Use different coloured pens for highlighting different points.

35mm slide projector

This is very similar to using an OHP, except that the slides are more expensive to produce and a darkened room is needed for best effective use. A slide projector is very useful when presenting to a larger audience. Use the following guidelines:

- Make sure that everyone can see the screen.
- Test the projector before you start, including a spare bulb.
- Use bold text and colours if possible. Be careful not to make the slides too complex.
- Use your own cassette loader and number your slides.
- Write notes, double-spaced and in capitals, using one page per slide. This way you can turn your pages in time with the slides.
- Change slides sparingly; too many slides can give people headaches.
- Keep messages short.
- As you will almost certainly need to dim or turn off the lighting, bear in mind that participants will find it difficult to make notes or ask questions.
- Make good use of graphs, diagrams and pictures which can be especially effective in this format as the colours are often very strong.

Computer projection panels

These are becoming more common and give you the opportunity to develop and deliver good-quality and slick presentations. Key points to note are as follows:

- Check and double-check all your graphics and software. Always carry back-ups with you.
- Double-check the operations of the equipment that you will be using in advance.

Presentation preparation worksheet

Background 1. What is the topic of your presentation? 2. What is the date and time of the presentation? 3. How long is the presentation? 4. Where is the presentation? 5. Who is the point of contact?	
Step 1: What are the objectives?	
Step 2: Who is the audience?	
Step 3: What is the most logical sequence to use for structuring the main body? • Chronological order • Topical approach • Problem/solution • Outlining • Priority • Spatial arrangement • Who, what, where, when, why, how	
Step 4: What are the main ideas?	Idea 1: Idea 2: Idea 3: Idea 4: Idea 5:

Reproduced from *50 Ways to Liven Up Your Meetings*, Graham Roberts-Phelps, Gower, Aldershot

Step 5: What information will support the main ideas?	
For idea 1:	
For idea 2:	
For idea 3:	
For idea 4:	
For idea 5:	
Step 6: What key points will make the opener a persuasive one?	
Step 7: What transitions will connect the opener to the main ideas and the main ideas to the close?	
Step 8: What key points will make the close a persuasive one?	

Using the '50 Ways' in meetings

Using the techniques and ideas in this book can be very straightforward if you follow this simple method:

1. First, highlight the benefits of the technique to the participants. Give them a reason why they should contribute – state what they will gain or learn.
2. If this is not apparent from step 1, state the purpose or objective of the meeting and discuss how the technique will help.
3. Explain the complete procedure or outline for the technique. This can be done either verbally, or by using an OHP (better) or a handout (better still).
4. Check for understanding before proceeding. Be sure to look around the room for confirming nods, and prompt if anybody is looking a little uncertain or confused.
5. Get started but monitor reactions carefully. Make yourself available to deal with questions as they arise, and move people from one technique to the next as time allows, or as they complete each section.

Because the session is shaped and defined by the participants, each time you use a technique it will work slightly differently. This is to be encouraged, as it ensures that the participants are actively contributing. However, it does mean that you have to stay alert as to whether all the meeting objectives are being met and be ready to deal with any issues or questions that may arise and so on.

The 12 applications

Each idea or activity has a list of suggested applications which can be briefly categorized under the situations detailed below. Most of the exercises have multiple applications; this gives you the flexibility to handle any individual meeting situations or issue.

Bringing the meeting alive

Energy levels are very important for a productive meeting. At times, you'll need to reinvigorate people, particularly at the start of a meeting or if the meeting is a long one. At other times, you may need to give people a break and a chance to clear their heads, before you move on to another topic. Look for:

1. Energizer
2. Icebreaker
3. Interlude

Helping the group work together

Good creative meetings happen when there is rapport between everyone involved, when they are communicating and working well together. These are processes that you need to be alert to; if things aren't going well, a well-chosen exercise can help the meeting members understand what's going wrong and work to put them right. Look for:

4. Building rapport
5. Encouraging communication
6. Practising group-working

Creativity and problem solving

Tackling problems or generating ideas within the meeting requires the right environment and a particular set of skills. Look for:

7. Encouraging creativity
8. Data analysis and problem-solving

Focusing on outcomes

Any meeting is only as productive as the results that it produces and it's important to keep your eyes fixed on what you want the meeting to achieve. Look for:

9. Controlling the meeting
10. Focusing individuals
11. Planning improvements
12. Testing learning.

How to really liven up your next meeting!

- Act like a game show host (your least favourite!) – award points every time someone speaks or contributes a good idea.
- Take all the chairs out and hold the meeting standing up.
- Shout 'Crackerjack' every time somebody agrees with or suggests a good idea.
- Get everyone to wear sunglasses throughout the meeting.
- Replace the chairs with deckchairs, have two tons of sand delivered and make everyone turn up in their beach gear, play Beach Boys songs and serve ice-creams and fizzy drinks. (Yes, this has actually happened!)
- Play LOUD music at the beginning and end of every session – make people dance in and out of the room.
- Write a company song.
- Sing the company song.
- Deliver your presentation in Rap.
- Give out whistles or hooters that people must use immediately they hear 'management speak' or waffle.
- Have a karaoke coffee-break.
- Seat participants in an unusual order:

  - by age
  - alphabetically
  - birthdate in the year
  - height
  - shoe size
  - amount or length of hair
  - zodiac signs
  - length of time with the organization

- Buy everyone an ice-cream instead of biscuits.
- Hold the meeting in a lift/cupboard/coach/plane/ airport lounge.
- Hold the meeting in McDonald's (free coffee refills).

- Hold a juggling competition.
- Hold an impressions competition.
- Play charades
- Use a sandglass egg-timer to 'time-out' talkative participants.
- Fine people for being late.
- End the meeting on time – just walk away.
- Respond to every sentence that someone says with 'That's easy for you to say ... '.
- Respond to every sentence that someone says with 'Aahh, you would say that ...'
- Start every sentence with 'Click, click, whirr ...'.
- Now the ideas are just getting silly! ...

Part II

50 ways to liven up your meetings

1 Are you thorough?

Suggested applications
- Ice-breaker
- Building rapport
- Practising group-working
- Encouraging creativity

What happens   Participants work carefully to count the dots in the designated areas to test their powers of accuracy and observation.

Purpose   To sharpen thinking and introduce people to working in pairs or small groups.

Format   Pairs/individual.

Resources   A copy of the handout for each participant.

Time   10–15 minutes or as required.

Procedure
1. Distribute a copy of the handout to each participant, explaining that accuracy is more important than speed in this case.
2. Ask everyone to work either individually or in pairs and carefully count the dots in the designated areas, writing their answers in the boxes beside each question. Allow 3 minutes or as long as it takes:
3. Give out the answers as follows:

    Q1.   25
    Q2.   18
    Q3.   19
    Q4.   11
    Q5.   2
    Q6.   5
    Q7.   5
    Q8.   4

Q9.   73
Q10.   27
(**Note**: Part dots are not counted.)

4. Allocate two points for each correct answer – the higher the score the better! Rate as follows:

Excellent   16–20
Good   10–15
Wake up!   Less than 10

Discussion points

- How did you tackle the task?
- Did you change the method you used from one question to the next?

Are you thorough?

Accuracy is more important than speed in this exercise. Carefully count the dots in the designated areas, and write your answers in the boxes beside each question. You have 3 minutes to complete this task.

How many dots are there?

1. In the squares – but not in the triangle, circle or rectangle? ☐

2. In the circle – but not in the triangle, square or rectangle? ☐

3. In the triangle – but not in the circle, square or rectangle? ☐

4. In the rectangle – but not in the triangle, circle or square? ☐

5. Common to the triangle and circle – but not in the rectangle or square? ☐

6. Common to the square and triangle – but not in the rectangle or circle? ☐

7. Common to the square and circle – but not in the triangle or rectangle? ☐

8. Common to the square and rectangle – but not in the circle or triangle? ☐

9. Common to the circle, square, triangle and rectangle? ☐

10. In the circle and the rectangle, but not the triangle. ☐

Your score ☐

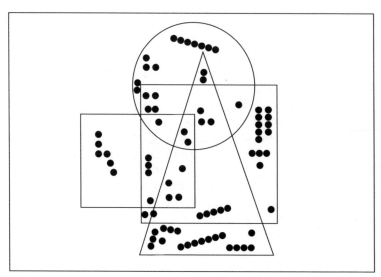

Reproduced from *50 Ways to Liven Up Your Meetings*, Graham Roberts-Phelps, Gower, Aldershot

2   A to Z

Suggested applications
- Ice-breaker
- Building rapport
- Practising group-working
- Encouraging creativity

What happens   Participants work in pairs to think of a named item for each letter of the alphabet. A range of topics can be used.

Purpose   To practise quick thinking and raise energy levels in a group.

Format   Pairs.

Resources   A pen and paper for each participant.
A flipchart and marker pens (optional).

Time   5–10 minutes.

Procedure   1. Ask the participants to work in pairs on this activity, which will test their quick thinking, extent of word usage or vocabulary, and their imagination.
2. Introduce the activity by explaining that our ability to express our ideas and interpret our words in an imaginative way can help us communicate better. Human beings who have the gift of speaking have at their disposal a rich and varied vocabulary as well as the knowledge of where and when to use words. They can find the word that expresses the exact shade of meaning that they wish to convey.
3. Next, select one or more of the words or categories listed (these can be written on a flipchart if preferred) and ask the pairs to compile a list of 26 related words beginning with each letter of the alphabet in alphabetical order. For example:

- Occupations   architect, baker, chemist …
- Cities   Albuquerque, Brussels, Cairo …
- Musical instruments   accordion, banjo, cello …
- Animals   aardvark, bear, camel …
- Foods   artichoke, bread, cranberry …

4. Allow 3 minutes for this task.
5. Run a brief discussion using the discussion points below.

Discussion points

- Did it surprise you how many different words you could generate?
- How much variety do we actually use in our conversation, compared to the richness we could use?

Variation   Ask the participants to compile similar lists from their own special field of interest, such as the names of plants, insects, pop songs or streets, countries, cities, towns, products, authors, books, television programmes, forms of transport and so forth.

3 Bars of soap

Suggested applications

- Energizer
- Interlude

What happens
Two volunteers read out a script. The rest of the group listen and enjoy the story as it unfolds.

Purpose
To provide an entertaining break and to illustrate how easily misunderstandings can occur!

Format
Main group.

Resources
Two copies of the handout.

Time
5–10 minutes.

Procedure
1. Ask for two volunteers. Invite them to the front of the room and give each a copy of the handout. Allocate one volunteer to read the customer role and the other to read the maid/hotel responses (which are in italics).
2. Explain to the rest of participants that they are about to hear an exchange of correspondence which actually took place between a guest at a London Hotel and a member of its staff. Ask them to listen and enjoy!

Bars of soap

Dear Maid, Please do not leave any more of those little bars of soap in my bathroom since I have brought my own bath-sized Dial. Please remove the six unopened little bars from the shelf under the medicine chest and another three in the shower soap dish. They are in my way. Thank you, S. Berman

Dear Room 635, I am not your regular maid. She will be back tomorrow, Thursday, from her day off. I took the 3 hotel soaps out of the shower soap dish as you requested. The 6 bars on your shelf I took out of your way and put on top of your Kleenex dispenser in case you should change your mind. This leaves only the 3 bars I left today according to my instructions from the management to leave 3 soaps daily. I hope this is satisfactory. Kathy, Relief Maid

Dear Maid, I hope you are my regular maid. Apparently Kathy did not tell you about my note to her concerning the little bars of soap. When I got back to my room this evening I found you had added 3 little Camays to the shelf under my medicine cabinet. I am going to be here in the hotel for two weeks and have brought my own bath-sized Dial so I won't need those 6 little Camays which are on the shelf. They are in my way when shaving, brushing teeth, etc. Please remove them. S. Berman

Dear Mr Berman, My day off was last Wednesday so the relief maid left 3 hotel soaps as instructed by the management. I took the 6 soaps which were in your way on the shelf and put them in the soap dish where your Dial was. I put the Dial in the medicine cabinet for your convenience. I didn't remove the 3 complimentary soaps which are always placed inside the medicine cabinet for all new check-ins and which you did not object to when you checked in last Monday. Please let me know if I can be of further assistance. Your regular maid, Dotty

Dear Mr Berman, The assistant manager, Mr Kensedder, informed me this morning that you called him last evening and said you were unhappy with your maid service. I have assigned a new girl to your room. I hope you will accept my apologies for any past inconvenience. If you have any future complaints please contact me so I can give it my personal attention. Call extension 1108 between 8am and 5pm. Thank you. Elaine Carmen, Housekeeper

cont'd

Reproduced from *50 Ways to Liven Up Your Meetings*, Graham Roberts-Phelps, Gower, Aldershot

Dear Mrs Carmen, It is impossible to contact you by phone since I leave the hotel for business at 7.45am and don't get back before 5.30 or 6pm. That's the reason I called Mr Kensedder last night. You were already off duty. I only asked Mr. Kensedder if he could do anything about those little bars of soap. The new maid you assigned me must have thought I was a new check-in today, since she left another 3 bars of hotel soap in my medicine cabinet along with her regular delivery of 3 bars on the bathroom shelf. In just 5 days here I have accumulated 24 little bars of soap. Why are you doing this to me? S. Berman

Dear Mr Berman, Your maid, Kathy, has been instructed to stop delivering soap to your room and remove the extra soaps. If I can be of further assistance, please call extension 1108 between 8am and 5pm. Thank you, Elaine Carmen, Housekeeper

Dear Mr Kensedder, My bath-sized Dial is missing. Every bar of soap was taken from my room including my own bath-sized Dial. I came in late last night and had to call the bellhop to bring me 4 little Cashmere Bouquets. S. Berman

Dear Mr Berman, I have informed our housekeeper, Elaine Carmen, of your soap problem. I cannot understand why there was no soap in your room since our maids are instructed to leave 3 bars of soap each time they service a room. The situation will be rectified immediately. Please accept my apologies for the inconvenience. Martin L. Kensedder, Assistant Manager

Dear Mrs Carmen, Who the hell left 54 little bars of Camay in my room? I came in last night and found 54 little bars of soap. I don't want 54 little bars of Camay. I want my one damn bar of bath-sized Dial. Do you realize I have 54 bars of soap in here. All I want is my bath-sized Dial. Please give me back my bath-sized Dial. S. Berman

Dear Mr Berman, You complained of too much soap in your room so I had them removed. Then you complained to Mr Kensedder that all your soap was missing so I personally returned them. The 24 Camays which had been taken and the 3 Camays you are supposed to receive daily. I don't know anything about the 4 Cashmere Bouquets. Obviously your maid, Kathy, did not know I had returned your soaps so she also brought 24 Camays plus the 3 daily Camays. I don't know where you got the idea this hotel issues bath-sized Dial. I was able to locate some

cont'd

bath-sized Ivory which I left in your room. Elaine Carmen Housekeeper

Dear Mrs Carmen, Just a short note to bring you up to date on my latest soap inventory. As of today I possess:

- On shelf under medicine cabinet: 18 Camay in 4 stacks of 4 and 1 stack of 2.
- On Kleenex dispenser: 11 Camay in 2 stacks of 4 and 1 stack of 3.
- On bedroom dresser: 1 stack of 3 Cashmere Bouquet, 1 stack of 4 hotel-size Ivory, and 8 Camay in 2 stacks of 4.
- Inside medicine cabinet: 14 Camay in 3 stacks of 4 and 1 stack of 2.
- In shower soap dish: 6 Camay, very moist.
- On north-east corner of bathtub: 1 Cashmere Bouquet, slightly used.
- On north-west corner of bathtub: 6 Camays in 2 stacks of 3.

Please ask Kathy when she services my room to make sure the stacks are neatly piled and dusted. Also, please advise her that stacks of more than 4 have a tendency to tip. May I suggest that my bedroom window sill is not in use and will make an excellent spot for future soap deliveries. One more item, I have purchased another bar of bath-sized Dial which I am keeping in the hotel vault in order to avoid further misunderstandings. S. Berman

Reproduced from *50 Ways to Liven Up Your Meetings*, Graham Roberts-Phelps, Gower, Aldershot

4   Be an author

Suggested applications
- Encouraging creativity
- Ice-breaker
- Focusing individuals

What happens

Participants work individually to create a narrative in a number of stages. After each stage, they pass on what they have written to their neighbour.

Purpose

To sharpen thinking and get participants working in pairs or small groups.

Format

Individual with group summary.

Resources

Eight sheets of paper plus a pen or pencil for each participant.

Time

45 minutes (but see 'Facilitator's notes').

Procedure

1. Give each individual eight sheets of paper and a pencil or pen.
2. Explain that a story is to be created and decide, with the group, whether it will be a tale of romance and adventure, or a mystern yarn and so on.
3. Agree, with the group, the names for hero, heroine and villain.
4. When the signal to start is given, each participant must write a paragraph or so, describing the background of the tale and the setting into which they wish first to place their hero.
5. When everyone has finished, ask them to put their topmost sheet (on which they have written) to the bottom of their pile, and pass that pile to the player on their left whereupon all must be ready for the next page of the narrative.
6. The stages of the narrative are as follows. Each stage should be started on a fresh sheet of paper.

- The background and setting.
- A description of the hero, with a brief description of his character.
- His purpose in undertaking an adventure, his destination and what he expects to find there.
- His journey through hostile regions; his battles with monsters and the like and the opportunities he grasps to perform good deeds.
- His discovery of ladies in distress; their beauty and virtue.
- His bold exploits in rescuing her from the clutches of the villain; his horrible practices which contrast with the ethics of the hero; how the ladies are eventually released and the villain thwarted!
- The triumphal return of the hero and heroine; the gratification of the hero's father and mother.
- A moral conclusion.

Of all these, the last item is, of course, the most important, and the participants may regard it as of sufficient gravity that they defer its completion until the remainder of the tales are read as a whole.

7. Ask the participants to read each of their stories aloud.

Facilitator's notes   This exercise is improved by keeping the participants working quickly, so set a time limit that is shorter than comfortable. 45 minutes is about right, but this may be varied accordingly.

Discussion points
- Which was judged to be the best narrative and why?
- Is there any similarity between the various tales? If so, in what ways are they similar?

5   Bingo quiz

Suggested applications
- Ice-breaker
- Energizer
- Testing learning

What happens
  Participants work individually, competing in the group, to answer questions to complete their bingo cards

Purpose
  To break the ice between people who may not know each other at the start of a meeting. Also useful as a device for ending a meeting on a high note.

Format
  Individual.

Resources
  A copy of the handout for each participant.
A selection of small prizes.

Time
  10–15 minutes or as required.

Procedure

1. Have available a supply of chocolate bars, or other small prizes for 'lines' and 'full houses'.
2. First distribute the handout and ask participants to place the nine dates anywhere on the grid. (This ensures a random element to the game.)
3. Explain that they are going to play a form of 'Bingo' and should raise their hands when they have completed a line or have a full house.
4. Next, select at random and read out one question at a time, making sure that participants write their answer in the corresponding square if they have that question number in their box.
5. Whenever somebody has a line, stop and check that their answers are correct. The line is only valid if *all* the answers are correct. Award a small prize.
6. Continue until a full house is called, and again check the

answers first. The full house is only valid if *all* the answers are correct. If they are not, then continue.

7. End the game when a participant achieves a full house or all the questions have been read out. Award a prize to the winner.

8. Take a moment to read out the questions and answers so that participants can check their answers.

Tip! Read out the number of the question 'bingo' style – for example, 'garden gate – number eight'.

Questions and answers

1.	What year was the Great Fire of London?	1666
2.	In what year did Elvis die?	1977
3.	In what year did man set foot on the moon?	1969
4.	In what year did the battle of Waterloo take place?	1815
5.	When did the Berlin Wall come down?	1989
6.	In what year was J.F. Kennedy assassinated?	1963
7.	In what year was Nelson Mandela released from custody?	1990
8.	In what year was the US Watergate scandal uncovered?	1974
9.	In what year did England win the football World Cup?	1966
10.	In what year did Sir Edmund Hillary and Sherpa Tenzing reach the summit of Mount Everest?	1953
11.	In what year was the Titanic launched?	1911
12.	In what year was the Statue of Liberty presented to the USA by France?	1883

Variations
- Create your own bingo quiz using the same format.
- If using as the end of a meeting, use questions referring back to the meeting's content for added emphasis.

History bingo quiz

Please select and write nine of the following numbers anywhere in the grid.

1883, 1989, 1966, 1974, 1963, 1969, 1815, 1911, 1953, 1990, 1996, 1977

Questions will be selected at random and read out one at a time. If you believe that you have the answer to a question in your grid, please circle the answer and write the question number or event in that numbered square.

You should raise your hand when you have a line or a full house.

The line or full house is *only* valid if all the answers are correct.

6 Biscuit barrel baffler

Suggested applications
- Practising group-working
- Building rapport
- Data analysis and problem solving
- Encouraging communication

What happens   Participants work in pairs, to determine from which jar to take the biscuit.

Purpose   To practise creative and lateral thinking.

Format   Pairs.

Resources   A copy of the handout for each participant.
An OHP (optional).

Time   15–20 minutes or as required.

Procedure
1. Ask the participants to work in pairs on this exercise, which will test their lateral thinking ability and creativity.
2. Distribute a copy of the handout to each participant or display the puzzle as an OHP.
3. Allow 10–15 minutes and then go around the group asking them to read out their answers or conclusion.
4. Run a brief discussion on how people arrived at their answers.

The answer   Take a cookie from the peanut butter and oatmeal jar. Since the jars are labelled incorrectly, you will either get an oatmeal or peanut butter cookie. If you get an oatmeal cookie you label the peanut butter and oatmeal jar as oatmeal. What was labelled the peanut butter jar must then contain peanut butter and oatmeal cookies because we are told that the jars are all incorrectly labelled. What was originally labelled as the oatmeal jar must contain peanut butter cookies.

Discussion points
- How did you try to solve this puzzle?
- What made this puzzle particularly difficult?

Variation   Ask the participants to work on the problem in small groups, creating more of a group interaction and team-building exercise.

Biscuit barrel baffler

Task

Three biscuit jars are incorrectly labelled as 'Oatmeal', 'Peanut Butter' and 'Peanut Butter and Oatmeal'.

The jars are closed, so you can't see inside.

You must take one cookie from only one jar and then correctly label each jar.

Which jar do you take the biscuit from?

Reproduced from *50 Ways to Liven Up Your Meetings*, Graham Roberts-Phelps, Gower, Aldershot

7   Brainstorm

Suggested applications
- Data analysis and problem-solving
- Planning improvements
- Practising group-working
- Encouraging creativity
- Energizer

What happens
Participants work in small groups to brainstorm the trigger question. Their ideas are then discussed by the group as a whole.

Purpose
To generate practical ideas and suggestions to solve problems or make improvements.

Format
Small groups/main group discussion.

Resources
A flipchart plus plenty of flipchart pages and pens.

Time
20–30 minutes or as required, plus group review.

Introductory notes
This activity is useful as both a meeting energizer and ice-breaker or as a practical way of generating ideas and suggestions on, for example, how to improve standards or overcome specific problems or situations that may stand in the way of implementing improvements to working practices.

It is particularly suitable for supervisory or management-level staff who may be involved in initiating, implementing or maintaining policy and procedures.

Brainstorming is a very well-established and useful tool in developing new ideas, concepts and thought patterns, and can be used for virtually any topical subject. The key requirements are: an open environment where people can offer ideas freely, without fear of judgement, criticism or ridicule; enough time; enough people; enough flipchart paper; and enough focus.

The trigger question is usually critical in developing a good brainstorming session. It should highlight some shortfall, issue, problem or dilemma and ask how it could be improved by specific or predefined amounts. Examples might be:

- How could we reduce customer complaints by 50 per cent in the next three months?
- How can applications for registration be improved and take half the time they do now?
- How can we reduce costs by 10 per cent across all departments?
- How can we reduce staff turnover?
- How can we improve staff punctuality?
- How can we improve customer service in ways that the customer can measure and appreciate?
- How can we motivate people to do a better job?

Procedure

1. List the following instructions on the flipchart:

   - Work in a group.
   - Brainstorm solutions to the question/problem.
   - Aim for quantity of ideas – all suggestions count.
   - Work quickly and creatively.

2. Divide the participants into groups of 4–7 and select a 'prompter' for each group. Give a copy of the handout to each 'prompter'.
3. Provide each group with flipchart paper and pens.
4. Provide the brainstorming focus or trigger question.
5. Offer a prize for the team with the most ideas, reminding them that *any idea is a good idea*.
6. Allow the groups 20–30 minutes to brainstorm the issue or trigger question.
7. Review each group's ideas in turn or ask each group to present their 'best three ideas'.

Variations

- Run a warm-up brainstorming session for just ten minutes to give participants the opportunity to practise this way of thinking. A good example would be to ask them to list as many applications as they can for a common plastic credit card other than buying things. A group of 3–6 people given 10–15 minutes should be able to generate at least 30 ideas, many of which are probably far more common than you might imagine. Alternatively, you could introduce this exercise by running a lateral-thinking puzzle.
- Consider running 'Driving Forces' as a follow-up to 'Brainstorming' if you now wish to select the 'best' ideas from the session.

Brainstorming: prompter role

Your role as prompter is to facilitate a short brainstorming session focused on the topic below. It is important that you encourage as many ideas as possible, without judgement or criticism. The *evaluation* of ideas uses a different mental process that is usually not compatible with creative thinking. Make sure that everybody in your group contributes and that people do not begin to judge other people's ideas.

Brainstorming topic:

---

8   Bus journey

Suggested applications
- Energizer
- Practising group-working
- Data analysis and problem-solving

What happens
Participants work as a group to assimilate information about a busy bus journey during which many passengers get on and off.

Purpose
To sharpen thinking and practise working together.

Format
Main group discussion.

Resources
None.

Time
3–5 minutes, or as required.

Procedure
1. Ask the participants to pay careful attention and then begin to describe a bus journey – say, from Tring to London (you can use a local route), asking the participants to keep count of the passengers.
2. Continue in the following manner: 'The bus started from Tring with 29 passengers. At Berkhamstead 5 got out and 7 got in. At King's Langley 11 got in and 3 got out. At Watford 17 got out and 4 got in. At Edgeware 9 got in and 1 got out.' Continue to add any other stops you wish.
3. Now ask: '*How many times did the bus stop?*'

This is almost certain to catch out the mathematicians in the group!

9   Call in the consultants

Suggested applications
- Practising group-working
- Data analysis and problem-solving
- Planning improvements

What happens Participants work, either in the whole group or in a number of smaller groups, to brainstorm and ultimately solve problems generated by other groups.

Purpose For participants to practise their problem-solving ability around the theme of the meeting and to reach their own conclusions about ways of improving in any particular area.

Format Main group/small groups.

Resources A copy of the handout for each participant.
A flipchart and marker pens (optional).

Time 30–45 minutes or as required, plus group review.

Procedure
1. Divide the participants into small groups of 3–5, and ask each group to give itself a name – perhaps the name of a rather grand-sounding consultancy company.
2. Give a copy of the handout to each participant or display as an OHP slide.
3. Ask everyone to select a question, problem or concern that may prevent them or their group from carrying out their job more effectively. Alternatively, focus assignments on 'How to implement some of the ideas from the meeting'.
4. Set a time limit (5–10 minutes), and ask the groups to write their chosen problem on a card or piece of paper, trying to be as specific as possible.
5. After 10 minutes, or when everybody has finished, collect in all the problems or questions and redistribute them to different groups.

6. Tell the groups that they now have to find a solution to the problem or question. Allow about 20–30 minutes.
7. After 30 minutes, or when everyone has finished, ask each group to present their solution to the other groups, explaining the reasoning behind their proposal.

Discussion points

- Is it easier to be objective or creative when it is not your problem?
- Did working in a group provide a better or quicker solution?
- Do others have similar problems to you?

Consultant's review

Task

- First choose a problem, issue or challenge that may prevent you or your team from achieving results or working more effectively.
- Write this clearly on a card or in the space below
- Swap the problem with another group of consultants
- Spend 20 minutes discussing potential solutions to the challenge you receive in return.
- Report back when asked.

Notes

Reproduced from *50 Ways to Liven Up Your Meetings*, Graham Roberts-Phelps, Gower, Aldershot

10   Change planner

Suggested applications
- Data analysis and problem-solving
- Planning improvements
- Focusing individuals

What happens   Working either individually or in pairs, participants use a structured four-point planner to help them understand and identify the issues around any major change in the organization.

Purpose   To help participants face and plan change constructively and positively.

Format   Individual/pairs

Resources   A flipchart. Flipchart paper and pens for each individual.
A copy of the handout for each participant (optional).

Time   20–45 minutes, or as required.

Introductory notes   Change today is commonplace in almost every organization, large and small. Observers and psychologists have noted that the human condition resists change, almost irrationally. 'Better the devil you know than the devil you don't know' is an attitude of mind that many people – indeed, most of us – will experience from time to time. This activity asks participants to focus on this change, or one aspect of change, and work through it in a practical and positive manner.

The chosen topic could be one of many, ranging from imposed change due to reorganization or personal change, for whatever reason. For example, this activity can be used when discussing actions arising from an earlier decision taken at the meeting. This might focus on some aspect of impending change that participants or attendees will have to face, such as the introduction of new technology, moving to a new job, taking on new responsibilities and so on.

The activity can also be useful in helping people to come to terms with change, encouraging them to break the change process down into a series of manageable steps and helping reduce any resistance to it.

Procedure
1. Draw the table presented in the following handout onto the flipchart.
2. Ask everyone to work either individually or in pairs and select changes arising from the meeting or session. Alternatively, select the change issue for discussion yourself.
3. Distribute a copy of the handout to each participant for making notes plus a sheet of flipchart paper and pens.
4. Ask the participants to list points under the headings in the boxes and prepare to present their chart. Allow 15–20 minutes or as required.
5. Ask each individual or pair to present their chart to the other members of the meeting.

Facilitator's notes

Following on from this activity, you could ask the participants to return to their pairs, choose one or more of the likely obstacles and develop a series of ideas or actions that could help prevent or overcome them.

If the group has listed more concerns than benefits, or more obstacles than milestones, once again it might be worth redirecting them, either through general discussion or by forming them back into groups to achieve more of a balance.

Discuss, as a group summary, how we resist change, often unconsciously coming up with reasons and excuses why not to change, even though we know it might be good for us and we know that, once we have a new perspective, we will gain new benefits.

Highlight examples of your own – situations when you have perhaps changed or developed and how this has helped you. These might include moving house, changing careers, moving jobs and so on.

Variation

You may want to vary the headings in each of the four boxes depending on the type of change. For example, when implementing a personal change generated by individuals the headings might read 'Key milestones', 'Likely obstacles', 'What's stopping me?', 'What can help me?'.

Change planner

Task

- Work individually or in pairs.
- Consider something that you would like to change or improve.
- Make notes in each of the four boxes to help you organize your thoughts and ideas.
- Present back when asked.

Change topic: _____

Key milestones in the process	Likely obstacles to the process
Benefits of the change	**People's concerns about the process**

11   Coat of arms

Suggested applications
- Focusing individuals
- Building rapport
- Practising group-working
- Energizer

What happens

Participants work individually using the specification list to design their own coat of arms. The rest of the group then have to match the coat of arms to its owner.

Purpose

To introduce participants or to develop rapport further in a group context. Also to practise the skills of self-disclosure.

Format

Individual/main group.

Resources

A copy of the handout for each participant.

Time

20–30 minutes.

Procedure

1. Distribute a copy of the handout to each participant and ask them to write down their answers to the seven questions in the relevant sections of the coat of arms. Allow 10–15 minutes.
2. Stress that the participants must not write their names on the sheet.
3. After the time has elapsed, redistribute the handouts so that no participant receives their own, but they also do not know whose handout they have.
4. Ask the participants to guess whose handout they have, based on the answers given, and to write this name on the top of the page.
5. Review the answers with the group as a whole, discussing both why they identified a certain individual and perhaps also the answers on the handouts.

Discussion points

- What clues were contained in the answers?

Coat of arms

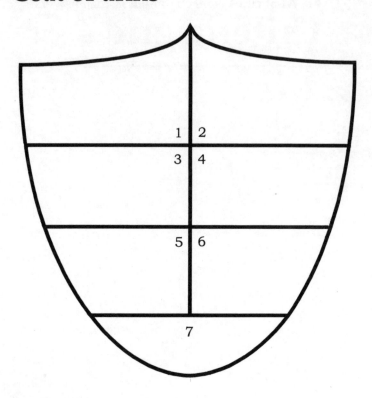

- In section 1, list two things you do very well.
- In section 2, write your personal maxim or motto.
- In section 3, list one thing on which you like to receive compliments.
- In section 4, list the three individuals who have influenced you most.
- In section 5, list the one thing about you that you would change if you could.
- In section 6, list the two major goals you have for the next two years.
- In section 7, write down one word that describes you.

12   Criteria grid

Suggested applications
- Focusing individuals
- Practising group-working
- Data analysis and problem-solving

What happens   Participants work in small groups to determine a subject for study and the key features relating to it. Then, as a whole group, they rate and discuss these features.

Purpose   To decide on, or examine, more complex issues such as quality processes, standards, product design, job specification or anything that involves balancing several important variables.

Format   Small groups/main group discussion.

Resources   A flipchart.
Flipchart paper and pens for each group.

Time   20–45 minutes or as required.

Introductory notes   This activity is particularly suitable for complex issues for which an analytical or detailed approach is required – for example, the criteria or measures for quality of customer service standards, deciding on priorities and job responsibilities, allocating work and project tasks, allocating and deciding on budget priorities.

It is important that enough time is spent not only on running the activity, but also on discussing the outcomes and any differences of opinion that may arise.

Procedure
1. Draw the criteria grid, given on the handout, on a flipchart.
2. Define variables for the elements A–G that you are comparing – for example, factors in choosing a venue for a conference (more criteria may be added as required). Try to limit the elements to six or seven key issues. Remember that the more elements you have the more complex the model

may become and the more issues will have to be discussed.

3. Divide the participants into small groups and supply each group with flipchart paper and pens, plus a copy of the handout.

4. Ask the groups to assess the elements against each other and indicate which they feel to be more important – for example, 'Is good parking (A) more or less important than leisure facilities (B)?'. **Write the letter of the *most* important factor in the box**. Total the number of times each element appears in the box.

5. Review and discuss with the whole group.

Variations
- Instead of choosing the elements and deciding what the critical factors are yourself, first ask the participants to decide the top six or seven key elements involved in the application they are considering.
- Have each group present their conclusions to the rest of the group and invite comment and discussion. Display all the completed pages around the room and highlight any discrepancies or patterns that may exist. Re-form the groups and ask them to reconsider or change any of their ratings following the main group discussion and to arrive at a definitive model.
- Discuss how they adapted their thoughts and attitudes through group discussion, if at all.

Criteria grid

First, list the six or seven most important criteria or considerations in assessing something or making a decision. Label these A–G or as many as you have.

Next, assess each element relative to each other and mark the most important in the box – for example, 'Which is more important, A or B?'. For instance, if you were choosing a conference venue, you might ask 'Is good parking (A) more or less important than leisure facilities (B)?' Write the letter of the **most important** factor in the box. Total the scores for each element.

	A	B	C	D	E	F	G
A	X						
B		X					
C			X				
D				X			
E					X		
F						X	
G							X

cont'd

Buying/choosing a car

Features/elements

A	=	fuel economy
B	=	sporting style
C	=	5 doors
D	=	air conditioning

	A	B	C	D	
A	X	A	C	A	Is A (fuel economy) more important than B, C, D?
B	A	X	C	B	Is B (sporty style) more important than B, C, D?
C	C	C	X	C	Is C (5 doors) more important than B, C, D?
D	A	B	C	X	Is D (air conditioning) more important than B, C, D?

Score

A	=	4 occurrences
B	=	2 occurrences
C	=	6 occurrences
D	=	0 occurrences

Priority

1 5 doors
2 good fuel economy
3 sporty style
4 air conditioning.

13   Currency quiz

Suggested applications
- Practising group-working
- Ice-breaker
- Energizer

What happens   Participants work in pairs to answer questions in a quiz. The correct answers are then reviewed against those they have given.

Purpose   To stretch memory and test general knowledge.

Format   Pairs.

Resources   A copy of the handout for each pair.
Two small prizes.

Time   10–15 minutes, or as required.

Procedure
1. Divide the participants into pairs and distribute a copy of the handout to each pair.
2. Set a time limit of, say, five minutes for the participants to supply the correct currency for each country listed.
3. Review the answers and award a small prize to the winning pair.

Currency quiz

Country	Currency
Austria	
Belgium	
Bulgaria	
Cyprus	
Czech	
Denmark	
England	
Finland	
France	
Germany	
Greece	
Hungary	
Iceland	
Italy	
Luxembourg	
Malta	
Monaco	
Netherlands	
Norway	
Poland	
Portugal	
Romania	
Russia	
Spain	
Sweden	
Turkey	
Vietnam	

Currency quiz: answers

Country	Currency
Austria	schilling
Belgium	franc
Bulgaria	lev
Cyprus	pound
Czech	koruna
Denmark	kroner
England	pound
Finland	markka
France	franc
Germany	deutschmark
Greece	drachma
Hungary	forint
Iceland	krona
Italy	lira
Luxembourg	franc
Malta	maltese pound
Monaco	franc
Netherlands	guilder
Norway	krone
Poland	zloty
Portugal	escudo
Romania	leu
Russia	rouble
Spain	peseta
Sweden	krona
Turkey	lira
Vietnam	dong

Reproduced from *50 Ways to Liven Up Your Meetings*, Graham Roberts-Phelps, Gower, Aldershot

14   Customer charter

Suggested applications
- Practising group-working
- Data analysis and problem-solving
- Planning improvements
- Testing learning

What happens   Participants work in small groups to study a specific work standard. Each group then sets out what the principle means, how it will be achieved and what its implications are.

Purpose   To assist with the development and clarification of an organization's or department's customer service charter or standards.

Format   Small groups.

Resources   A flipchart.
Flipchart paper and pens for each group.
A copy of the handout for each participant.

Time   20–45 minutes, or as required.

Introductory notes   This activity is of particular use in meetings concerning customer service or quality ('customer' can, of course, be an internal customer as well as an external one).

It is a good idea, before the meeting, to collect some customer charters from your own or related businesses. Many hotels, restaurants, banks and public utilities have leaflets defining their customer standards. Read this out and review them as a way of introducing this activity.

This activity can also be used to define standards of teamwork, communication, meeting guidelines, purchasing procedures and the internal standards or functions of a particular support department or team.

Procedure   1.   Write the title of the activity on a flipchart.

2. Divide the participants into small groups of 4–6 and supply each group with flipchart paper and pens.
3. Provide an example or model of a customer charter, and make sure that everyone understands the concept.
4. Distribute a copy of the handout to each participant for information.
5. Ask the groups to write a 'customer charter' on the flipchart paper, defining the rights, standards and minimum expectations for a given group of 'customers'. Encourage the participants to word each element or statement in a way that is clear, focused and precise in its definition. Allow 15–20 minutes, or as much time as is required.
6. Post the flipchart pages around the room and ask each group to present their charter.
7. Run a discussion on the issues and ideas with the whole group.

Variations
- Prior to the meeting, or following this activity, ask the 'customers' who are being focused on in this session to compile their own 'customer charter' of what they would like to have as standards and expectations. Match this with the charters developed during the meeting to see how similar they are.

  A personnel department, for example, may have its own definition of the service which it believes it can offer to other managers and staff within an organization. This definition may be very different to the expectations of the staff and managers.
- Following the group discussion, ask everyone to return to their groups and edit and review their customer charter based on the points made during the group discussion and any observations that may have come from their 'customers'.
- Following the group review session, run a short exercise asking the participants to discuss how the customer charter may be implemented, or how the standards can be guaranteed, or indeed what recourse customers may have if the standards are not achieved. This will also make sure that the standards specified are measurable.
- An alternative discussion may be structured around how you can avoid this customer charter becoming not just pleasant platitudes and well-meaning intentions, but a real and practical way of delivering customer satisfaction.

Customer charter

Task

- Work in a small group.
- Write a 'customer charter' defining the rights and standards customers can expect to receive
- Present back when asked.

Guidelines

Standards and rights should be:

- **Clearly defined** – in terms everyone can understand
- **Measurable** – so that you can identify when or how well you are achieving each one
- **Achievable** – it's counterproductive to specify standards or rights that you have no chance of achieving
- **Relevant** – make sure that each element in the charter has a purpose which you are able to explain. There's no point in doing things 'for their own sake', however laudable they may be.

Notes

15   Definitely speaking

Suggested applications
- Data analysis and problem-solving
- Encouraging creativity
- Encouraging communication

What happens   Participants work in pairs or individually to study a list of sentences and rewrite them so that they have a definite meaning.

Purpose   To sharpen thinking and written expression and to get participants working in pairs or small groups.

Format   Individual/pairs.

Resources   A copy of the handout for each participant.

Time   10–15 minutes, or as required.

Procedure
1. Distribute a copy of the handout to each participant and read through the instructions.
2. Ask everyone to work individually or in pairs and set a time limit, of say, 10 minutes.
3. When the time is up, or when most participants have finished, review answers with the whole group. Whilst many people will recognize, and enjoy, the humour involved in vague and ambiguous statements, they will also realize how easy it is to be unclear.

Definitely speaking

Rewrite the following statements and phrases so that they mean something definite. You may have to invent some information to make some of them definite.

1. We should give full details perhaps in writing.

2. The committee will continue to meet on an ongoing basis.

3. In the not too distant future.

4. The workers have got to like the new shift system.

5. The cost may be upwards of a figure rather below £10 million.

6. There is no reason to doubt that it is not true.

7. He told the operator that the supervisor was surprised by what he had said to him.

8. Time will not be wasted calling on small accounts.

9. A discussion was held on overtime working in the conference room.

10. Downtime has been reduced to a minimum.

11. We cannot employ too many marketing consultants under present conditions.

12. They ignored the advice of the committee which was very foolish.

16   Devising mentally

Suggested applications
- Ice-breaker
- Energizer
- Encouraging creativity

What happens   Participants work individually or in pairs to build phrases from the lists of words given.

Purpose   To practise concentration skills.

Format   Individual/pairs.

Resources   A copy of the handout for each participant.

Time   10–15 minutes, or as required.

Procedure   1.   Distribute a copy of the handout to each participant.
2.   Ask them to work individually or in pairs to complete the exercise. Allow 10–15 minutes.
3.   Review the answers (see below).

Answers
- Lock-up garage
- Brake horsepower
- Three-core cable
- Plaster of paris
- Rack-and-pinion
- Workmanship
- Threadbareness
- Butterfly-screw

Devising mentally

Take a word from each column and find eight words or phrases each of which is made up of three elements – for example, lock-up garage.

A	B	C
Plaster	Man	Garage
Rack	Bare	Power
Lock	Of	Ship
Work	Fly	Paris
Thread	Up	Cable
Brake	Core	Pinion
Butter	Horse	Ness
Three	And	Screw

17 Driving forces

Suggested applications
- Data analysis and problem-solving
- Planning improvements
- Testing learning

What happens Participants work in small groups to identify how employees, systems, the organizational culture and external forces can act as driving forces behind any changes or, equally, present obstacles or brakes to the process.

Purpose To identify and understand driving and restraining forces and to begin to devise strategies for maximizing driving forces and minimizing restraining forces.

Format Small groups.

Resources A copy of the handout for each participant (optional).
A flipchart and marker pens.

Time 20–45 minutes, or as required.

Introductory notes This activity is useful for tackling issues when introducing a plan for change, problem-solving, goal-setting or making improvements.

It is a well-documented fact that, in any change situation, there are two sets of forces at work. The driving force is striving for improvement or change and the restraining force is standing against that change or, in some way, holding back the progress. These forces may be present in people – who are in favour of, or totally opposed to, the change – or may be systems that cannot accommodate the new way of working.

This activity can be used in a wide range of different applications, and is ideal for meetings dealing with quality, customer service or management change initiative.

Procedure
1. Draw the chart on a flipchart or distribute a copy of the handout to each participant.
2. Organize the participants into small groups.
3. Lead a short discussion or presentation on how any change or improvement has two sets of forces. Highlight that these forces can be either external to, ourselves or the organization, or can be internal creations. Here are some examples that could be used to examine pushing and pulling driving forces: why customers change suppliers, reorganizing a department and changing a process or method.
4. Explain that this activity will allow the participants to identify what these are and begin to understand how they can be maximized or overcome.
5. Ask the participants to summarize the forces at work in a given situation as either driving forces (moving forward) or restraints (holding back)
6. Provide each group with flipchart paper and pens and allow them 15–20 minutes to complete the exercise.
7. Post the flipchart sheets around the room and ask each group to review them.
8. Run a discussion on how best to remove or reduce restraining forces.

Variations
- Ask the groups to prioritize the forces in terms of their likely effect and the ease or difficulty of changing them.
- Ask the participants to return to their groups to discuss ways of maximizing one or more driving forces and of overcoming the different restraining forces. Are these forces real or imagined?
- Ask the groups to consider what they can do now that they have identified these different forces.

Force field analysis

Identify the driving forces and restraining forces in the following situation:

Driving forces ⊃	⊂ Restraining forces

18   Figures of eight

Suggested applications
- Ice-breaker
- Energizer
- Data analysis and problem-solving

What happens   Participants work individually or in pairs to brainstorm a numerical puzzle.

Purpose   To sharpen thinking.

Format   Individual/pairs.

Resources   A copy of the handout for each participant.

Time   15–20 minutes, or as required.

Procedure
1. Distribute a copy of the handout to each participant and read through the instructions.
2. Ask them to work individually or in pairs to solve the problem and set a time limit of, say, 10 minutes.
3. When the time is up ask several volunteers for the answer, and check whether they are correct.

Answer $888 + 88 + 8 + 8 + 8 = 1000$

or

$8 \times 88 - 8 + 8 + 8 + 88 + 88 + 88 + 8 + 8 + 8 = 1000$

Figures of eight

The figure 8 is an interesting one. Numerologists know it as the Number of Justice. It is also sometimes known as the Number of Regeneration – have a look at the font the next time you enter an old church: the odds are that it will have an octagonal base.

Task

Here is a simple problem. What is the smallest number of figure eights needed to produce exactly one thousand. You can arrange them in any way you please, and use plus, minus, or multiplication signs if you want to. No other figures may be used.

How many other answers can you get of different lengths?

Reproduced from *50 Ways to Liven Up Your Meetings*, Graham Roberts-Phelps, Gower, Aldershot

19 Flowcharting

Suggested applications
- Testing learning
- Encouraging communication
- Building rapport

What happens
Participants work in pairs or small groups to develop a flowchart to illustrate the steps within a chosen work process.

Purpose
To summarize and check understanding of key processes, procedures or operations.

Format
Pairs/small groups.

Resources
A flipchart.
Flipchart paper and pens for each group.

Time
30–45 minutes, or as required.

Introductory notes
Flowcharting is a useful and valued visual way of organizing processes, thoughts and frequencies in any activity. It can be used in a variety of different situations and subjects – for example, in operating procedures, security checks, time management, customer service, problem-solving, and many other organizational areas, such as defining the credit control procedures.

You might choose to start the session by drawing some of the different flowcharting symbols on the flipchart and explaining their definition (see 'Facilitator's notes' below). Whilst rarely used outside technical scientific or computer fields, some of these symbols can be successfully and usefully adapted for this activity.

Procedure
1. Prepare a flipchart page as shown in 'Example Flowchart' on page 83.
2. Direct the participants – working in pairs or small groups –

to prepare a flowchart for a process, procedure or operation related to the meeting topic. Illustrate by means of a simple example – for instance, making a hot drink.

3. Supply each group with flipchart paper and pens and allow them 15–20 minutes or as much time as is needed to complete the task.

4. Post the flipchart pages around the room and ask the groups to present and review them.

Facilitator's notes

A flowchart is a visual representation of the sequence of the content of a process. It shows what action or event comes first, second, third, and so on, as well as what others need to do, if anything, and what will happen when they've done it.

A completed flowchart organizes topics, strategies, treatments and options into a plan from which the details of each stage or element can be worked out.

Essentially, it is a working map of the final process. However, the flowchart is not created in stone and will probably change as the details of the final process are worked through. The symbols commonly used in flowcharts are listed and described below.

- **Oval**. The oval (sometimes called the rounded rectangle) is used only at the beginning or at the end of a flowchart with the word 'start' or 'end' inside the oval.
- **Rectangle**. The rectangle is used for actions or steps – for example, 'Put the sugar in the coffee'.
- **Diamond**. Diamonds are used for decisions or questions – for example, 'Lemon or milk?'.
- **Circle**. Circles are the 'Go To' symbols and they are used when your flowchart gets too big for one sheet of paper (for example, 'Go to Page 2') or when your flowchart gets complicated and you want to avoid arrow lines that cross each other. If you use this symbol, you must have an exit point (for example, 'Go to A') and an entry point (a place to go marked 'A'). In the diagram below, the lower circle is the one that means 'Go to A', and the upper circle means 'Continue from here after leaving the other circle'.
- **Branching**. The diagrams on the following page show two different ways to show branching. One diagram is the typical way to show a question or decision that has two possible options (for example, 'yes', or 'no'). If you have three possible options, you can modify the diagram by adding a third arrow from the bottom point of the diamond shape. The other diagram shows how to handle multiple options. This structure is necessary if there are four or more options.

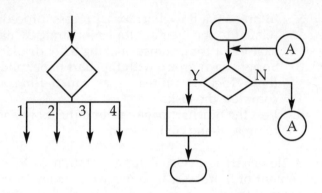

Variations
- If you have one large process with several steps – for example, processing an insurance claims form – you could break it down into different sections, allocating one to each pair or small group. Ask each group to identify the flow of information, paperwork and customer contact for each section.
- At the end of the exercise ask the groups to re-form to review their flowchart and create a new model, eliminating any unnecessary steps, simplifying procedures and speeding up certain tasks by running things in parallel.
- At the beginning of the exercise, it might be useful to discuss how this sequence or procedure came into being. Did it simply evolve over time or did somebody, in fact, sit down and design the optimum plan? (Most sequences or processes are a combination of the two.)

Example flowchart

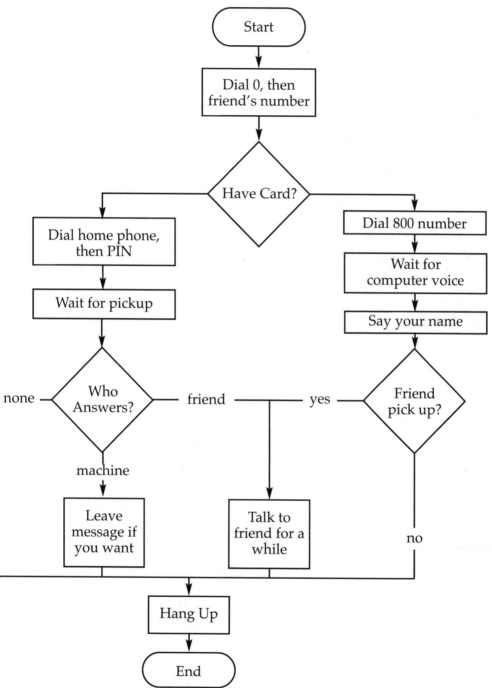

Reproduced from *50 Ways to Liven Up Your Meetings*, Graham Roberts-Phelps, Gower, Aldershot

20   Guess who?

Suggested applications
- Ice-breaker
- Energizer
- Building rapport
- Encouraging group-working

What happens   Participants work in small groups. Everyone completes a descriptive questionnaire, a spokesperson reads some of their responses and the rest of group have to guess to whom they relate.

Purpose   To introduce participants to other meeting members in an informal and interesting way.

Format   Small groups.

Resources   A copy of the handout for each participant.

Time   25–30 minutes, or as required.

Procedure

1. Distribute a copy of the handout to each participant. (If preferred it could be distributed, with the agenda, before the meeting.)
2. Ask the participants to take a few minutes to complete the statements, writing down their first or instinctive answers. **Do not explain the purpose or objective of this activity at this stage.**
3. Now ask the participants to work in small groups in separate rooms if possible, and to appoint a team leader or spokesperson. Each team leader has to collect up the questionnaires, shuffle them and give out clues, one from each sheet, with the rest of the team trying to guess who the person is from the clues or responses given. Allow 10–15 minutes, or until everybody has been identified.
4. When the time is up, ask the team leader of each group to

present in turn which responses gave people away, and which participants were the most difficult to identify.
5. Run a discussion on the points outlined under 'Discussion points' below.

Discussion points

- How did you approach the group discussion?
- What surprised you about other people's responses?
- What responses made it difficult to guess whose answer it was?
- How did you feel when your colleagues were right – or wrong – about the responses they attributed to you?

Variation   At step 3, collect up all the questionnaires yourself and run the activity with the group as a whole. Then, at step 4, allow an open discussion on the responses.

My favourite

Film is _____

Song is _____

Colour is _____

Sandwich filling is _____

Actor is _____

Book is _____

Magazine is _____

Daydream is _____

TV show is _____

Possession is _____

21   Human bingo

Suggested applications
- Ice-breaker
- Energizer
- Encouraging creativity

What happens   People work individually or in pairs to complete the bingo exercise, based on the characters of the other people in the meeting.

Purpose   To break the ice in a larger meeting or conference and to encourage participants to share information about each other in an informal, lighthearted and non-threatening manner. This activity is a good way to start a meeting, particularly where people may know each other and traditional ice-breakers are not really relevant.

Format   Individual/pairs.

Resources   A copy of the handout for each participant.

Time   10–15 minutes, or as required.

Procedure   1.   Distribute a copy of the handout to each participant.
2.   Tell the participants to circulate as quickly as they can and write one person in each box. Keep the exercise going until all, or nearly all, the participants have got a 'full house'.

Variation   You might want to include one or two red herrings that do not belong to anybody just to try to get people thinking.

📄 Human bingo

Circulate around the room and find the names of as many people as possible for each box. Write their name in the space provided.

Is over 6 feet tall	Speaks two languages	Has a tattoo
_____	_____	_____
Is bald (or nearly)	Drives a red car	Has run a marathon
_____	_____	_____
Can juggle or do a magic trick	Has a famous friend, or relative	Plays a musical instrument regularly
_____	_____	_____

22 Humorous interludes

Suggested applications
- Ice-breaker
- Energizer
- Building rapport

What happens
Participants share a series of comic or contradictory statements, laugh and reflect on our typically illogical approach to business.

Purpose
To liven up a meeting in an entertaining and unusual way or to re-energize and reconnect people after a long session and before continuing with more serious business.

Format
Main group discussion

Resources
OHP (optional).
Copies of the handout (optional).

Time
5 minutes, or as required.

Procedure
1. Read out, display on an OHP or circulate all or part of the following collection of humorous quotes and anecdotes.

Ways to handle stress

1. Jam 39 tiny marshmallows up your nose and try to sneeze them out.

2. Use your Mastercard to pay your Visa bill.

3. Pop some popcorn without putting the lid on.

4. When someone says 'Have a nice day', tell them you have other plans.

5. Make a list of things to do that you've already done.

6. Dance naked in front of your pets.

7. Put your toddler's clothes on backwards and send him off to playgroup as if nothing was wrong.

8. Retaliate for tax woes by filling out your tax forms with roman numerals

9. Tattoo 'OUT TO LUNCH' on your forehead.

10. Tape pictures of your boss on watermelons and launch them from high places.

11. Leaf through *National Geographic Magazine* and draw underwear on the natives.

12. Go shopping. Buy everything. Sweat in it. Return it the next day.

13. Pay your electric bill in pennies.

14. Drive to work in reverse.

15. Relax by mentally reflecting on your favourite episode of *The Flintstones* during that important finance meeting.

16. Refresh yourself: put your tongue on a cold steel guardrail.

17. Tell your boss to blow it out of his mule and let him figure it out.

18. Polish your car with ear wax.

19. Read the dictionary upside down and look for secret messages.

20. Write a short story, using Alphabet Spaghetti.

cont'd

21. Lie on your back eating celery ... using your navel as a salt dipper.

22. Make up a language and ask people for directions.

You know it is going to be a bad day when ...

- Every person you ask for job leads says 'I wish I had some job leads'.
- People in your department greet each other with 'How's the job search?' instead of 'How's it going?'.
- The bird singing outside your window is a buzzard.
- The gypsy fortuneteller offers to refund your money.
- There is a *60 Minutes* film crew at your office door.
- You call your answering service and they tell you it's none of your business.
- You find a completely empty car park when you get to work at 9.00 am.
- You find your boss, two higher levels of management, and a security guard waiting for you when you get in to work.
- You find your office door has disappeared since last night.
- You cut your finger on your 'get well' card.
- You are about to put on the clothes you wore home from the party and find there aren't any.
- You have to borrow from your Visa to pay off your Mastercard bill.
- You put both contact lenses in the same eye.
- You see the team from a consumer affairs TV programme waiting for you in your office.
- You see your picture at the post office with the caption '£100,000 Reward'.
- You turn on the news and they're displaying emergency routes out of your town.
- You wake up and your braces are locked together.
- You wake up face down on the pavement.

cont'd

Reproduced from *50 Ways to Liven Up Your Meetings*, Graham Roberts-Phelps, Gower, Aldershot

- You wake up to discover that your waterbed has split; then you remember that you don't have a waterbed.

- Your birthday cake collapses from the weight of the candles.

- Your boss tells you to not bother taking off your coat.

- Your car costs more to fill up than it did to buy.

- Your doctor tells you, 'Well, I have bad news and good news …'.

- Your four-year-old tells you that it is almost impossible to flush a grapefruit down the toilet.

- Your horn goes off accidentally and remains stuck as you follow a group of Hell's Angels on the motorway.

- Your income tax rebate cheque bounces.

- Your manager calls you into the office on a Friday.

- Your twin brother/sister forgets your birthday.

- Your wife says 'Good morning Bill', and your name is George.

Reproduced from *50 Ways to Liven Up Your Meetings*, Graham Roberts-Phelps, Gower, Aldershot

The truth about stress

Stress helps you seem important

> Anyone as stressed as you must be working very hard and, therefore, is probably doing something very crucial.

Stress helps you maintain personal distance and avoid intimacy

> Anyone as busy as you are certainly can't be expected to form emotional attachments to anyone. And let's face it, you're not much fun to be around anyway.

Stress helps you to avoid responsibilities

> Obviously you're too stressed to be given any more work. This gets you off the hook for all the mundane chores; let someone else take care of them.

Stress gives you a chemical rush

> Stress might be considered a cheap thrill, and you can give yourself a 'hit' any time you choose. But be careful, you might get addicted to your own adrenaline.

Stress helps you avoid success

> Why risk being 'successful' when by simply staying stressed you can avoid all of that? Stress can keep your performance level so low that success won't ever be a threat.

Stress lets you keep your authoritarian management style

> The authoritarian style of 'Just do what I say!' is generally permissible under crisis conditions. If you maintain a permanently stressed crisis atmosphere, you can justify an authoritarian style all the time.

How to successfully maintain your stress levels

> Are you worried now about how to stay stressed? You'll have no

cont'd

Reproduced from *50 Ways to Liven Up Your Meetings*, Graham Roberts-Phelps, Gower, Aldershot

trouble if you practise the following clinically proven methods:

- **Never exercise**. Exercise wastes a lot of time that could be spent worrying.
- **Eat anything you want**. Hey, if cigarette smoke can't cleanse your system, a balanced diet isn't likely to.
- **Gain weight**. Work hard at staying at least 25 pounds over your recommended weight.
- **Take plenty of stimulants**. The old standards – caffeine, nicotine, sugar and cola – will continue to do the job just fine.
- **Avoid 'New Age' practices**. Ignore the evidence suggesting that meditation, yoga, deep breathing, and/or mental imaging help reduce stress. The Protestant work ethic is good for everyone, Protestant or not.
- **Get rid of your social support system**. Let the few friends who are willing to tolerate you know that you concern yourself with friendships only if you have time, and you *never* have time. If a few people persist in trying to be your friend, avoid them.
- **Personalize all criticism**. Anyone who criticizes any aspect of your work, family, dog, house or car is mounting a personal attack. Don't take time to listen, be offended, then counter the attack!
- **Throw out your sense of humour**. Staying stressed is no laughing matter, and it shouldn't be treated as one.
- **Males and females alike, be macho and never, ever ask for help**. If you want it done right, do it yourself!
- **Become a workaholic**. Put work before everything else, and be sure to take work home evenings and weekends. Keep reminding yourself that vacations are for sissies.
- **Discard good time management skills**. Schedule in more activities every day than you can possibly get done and then worry about it all whenever you get a chance.
- **Procrastinate**. Putting things off to the last second always produces a marvellous amount of stress.
- **Worry about things you can't control**. Worry about the stock market, earthquakes, the approaching Ice Age – you know, all the big issues.
- **Become not only a perfectionist but also set impossibly high standards**. And either beat yourself up, or feel guilty, depressed, discouraged, and/or inadequate when you don't meet them.

Reproduced from *50 Ways to Liven Up Your Meetings*, Graham Roberts-Phelps, Gower, Aldershot

Procrastinator's creed

- I believe that if anything is worth doing, it would have been done already.

- I shall never move quickly, except to avoid more work or find excuses.

- I will never rush into a job without a lifetime of thought.

- I shall meet all of my deadlines directly in proportion to the amount of bodily injury I could expect to receive from missing them.

- I firmly believe that tomorrow holds the possibility for new technologies, astounding discoveries, and a reprieve from my obligations.

- I truly believe that all deadlines are unreasonable regardless of the amount of time given.

- I shall never forget that the probability of a miracle, though infinitely small, is not exactly zero.

- If at first I don't succeed, there is always next year.

- I shall always decide not to decide, unless of course I decide to change my mind.

- I shall always begin, start, initiate, take the first step, and/or write the first word, when I get around to it.

- I obey the law of inverse excuses which demands that the greater the task to be done, the more insignificant the work that must be done prior to beginning the greater task.

- I will never put off until tomorrow what I can forget about.

Reproduced from *50 Ways to Liven Up Your Meetings*, Graham Roberts-Phelps, Gower, Aldershot

'Oops, did I say that?'

'Computers in the future may weigh no more than 1.5 tons.'
(Popular Mechanics, forecasting the relentless march of science, 1949)

'I think there is a world market for maybe five computers.'
(Thomas Watson, chairman of IBM, 1943)

'I have travelled the length and breadth of this country and talked with the best people, and I can assure you that data processing is a fad that won't last out the year.'
(The editor in charge of business books for Prentice Hall, 1957)

'There is no reason anyone would want a computer in their home.'
(Ken Olson, president, chairman and founder of digital equipment corporations, 1977)

'This "telephone" has too many shortcomings to be seriously considered as a means of communication. The device is inherently of no value to us.'
(Western Union internal memo, 1876)

'The wireless music box has no imaginable commercial value. Who would pay for a message sent to nobody in particular?'
(David Sarnoff's associates in response to his urgings for investment in the radio in the 1920s)

'I'm just glad it'll be Clark Gable who's falling on his face and not Gary Cooper.'
(Gary Cooper on his decision not to take the leading role in *Gone With The Wind*)

'We don't like their sound, and guitar music is on the way out.'
(Decca Recording Co. rejecting the Beatles, 1962)

'640K ought to be enough for anybody.'
(Bill Gates, 1981)

Unusual job interviews

Personnel directors of the 100 largest corporations were asked to describe their most unusual experience interviewing prospective employees. Here is a selection.

- A job applicant challenged the interviewer to an arm wrestle.

- The interviewee wore a Walkman, explaining that she could listen to the interviewer and the music at the same time.

- The candidate fell and broke their arm during the interview.

- The candidate announced she hadn't had lunch and proceeded to eat a hamburger and french fries in the interviewer's office.

- The applicant said if he was hired he would demonstrate his loyalty by having the corporate logo tattooed on his forearm.

- The applicant interrupted the interview to phone her therapist for advice on how to answer specific interview questions.

- The candidate brought a large dog to the interview.

- The applicant refused to sit down and insisted on being interviewed standing up.

- The candidate dozed off during the interview.

Unusual job interview questions

- 'Why aren't you in a more interesting business?'
- 'What are the zodiac signs of all the board members?'
- 'Why do you want references?'
- 'Do I have to dress for the next interview?'
- 'I know this is off the subject, but will you marry me?'
- 'Will the company pay to relocate my horse?'
- 'Would it be a problem if I'm angry most of the time?'
- 'Does your company have a policy regarding concealed weapons?'
- Do you think the company would be willing to lower my pay?'
- 'Why am I here?'

📄 Signs

- *In a laundromat*:
  AUTOMATIC WASHING MACHINES: PLEASE REMOVE ALL YOUR CLOTHES WHEN THE LIGHT GOES OUT

- *In a London department store*:
  BARGAIN BASEMENT UPSTAIRS

- *In an office*:
  AFTER TEA BREAK STAFF SHOULD EMPTY THE TEAPOT AND STAND UPSIDE DOWN ON THE DRAINING BOARD

- *On a church door*:
  THIS IS THE GATE OF HEAVEN. ENTER YE ALL BY THIS DOOR. (THIS DOOR IS KEPT LOCKED BECAUSE OF THE DRAFT. PLEASE USE SIDE DOOR.)

- *Outside a secondhand shop*:
  WE EXCHANGE ANYTHING – BICYCLES, WASHING MACHINES ETC. WHY NOT BRING YOUR WIFE ALONG AND GET A WONDERFUL BARGAIN?

- *Sign outside a new town hall which was to be opened by the Prince of Wales*:
  THE TOWN HALL IS CLOSED UNTIL OPENING. IT WILL REMAIN CLOSED AFTER BEING OPENED. OPEN TOMORROW.

- *Outside a photographer's studio*:
  OUT TO LUNCH: IF NOT BACK BY FIVE, OUT FOR DINNER ALSO

- *Outside a disco*:
  SMARTS IS THE MOST EXCLUSIVE DISCO IN TOWN. EVERYONE WELCOME.

- *Warning of quicksand*:
  QUICKSAND. ANY PERSON PASSING THIS POINT WILL BE DROWNED. BY ORDER OF THE DISTRICT COUNCIL.

- *Notice sent to residents of a Wiltshire parish*:
  DUE TO INCREASING PROBLEMS WITH LITTER LOUTS AND VANDALS WE MUST ASK ANYONE WITH RELATIVES BURIED IN THE GRAVEYARD TO DO THEIR BEST TO KEEP THEM IN ORDER

cont'd

Reproduced from *50 Ways to Liven Up Your Meetings*, Graham Roberts-Phelps, Gower, Aldershot

- *In a dry cleaner's window*:
  ANYONE LEAVING THEIR GARMENTS HERE FOR MORE THAN 30 DAYS WILL BE DISPOSED OF

- *Sign on a motorway garage*:
  PLEASE DO NOT SMOKE NEAR OUR PETROL PUMPS. YOUR LIFE MAY NOT BE WORTH MUCH BUT OUR PETROL IS.

- *In a healthfood shop window*:
  CLOSED DUE TO ILLNESS

- *In a Safari park*:
  ELEPHANTS PLEASE STAY PUT IN YOUR CAR

- *In a conference venue*:
  FOR ANYONE WHO HAS CHILDREN AND DOESN'T KNOW IT, THERE IS A DAY CARE ON THE FIRST FLOOR

- *In a field*:
  THE FARMER ALLOWS WALKERS TO CROSS THE FIELD FOR FREE, BUT THE BULL CHARGES

- *On a leaflet*:
  IF YOU CANNOT READ, THIS LEAFLET WILL TELL YOU HOW TO GET LESSONS

- *On a repair shop door*:
  WE CAN REPAIR ANYTHING. (PLEASE KNOCK HARD ON THE DOOR – THE BELL DOESN'T WORK.)

- *At a Norfolk farm gate*:
  BEWARE! I SHOOT EVERY TENTH TRESPASSER AND THE NINTH ONE HAS JUST LEFT.

Reproduced from *50 Ways to Liven Up Your Meetings*, Graham Roberts-Phelps, Gower, Aldershot

Insurance claim forms

The following are actual statements found on insurance forms where car drivers attempted to summarize the details of an accident in the fewest possible words. The instances of faulty writing serve to confirm that even incompetent writing can be highly entertaining!

- Coming home I drove into the wrong house and collided with a tree I don't have.

- The other car collided with mine without giving warning of its intention.

- I thought my window was down, but I found it was up when I put my head through it.

- I collided with a stationary truck coming the other way.

- A truck backed through my windshield into my wife's face.

- The guy was all over the road. I had to swerve a number of times before I hit him.

- I pulled away from the side of the road, glanced at my mother-in-law and headed over the embankment.

- In an attempt to kill a fly I drove into a telephone pole.

- I had been shopping for plants all day and was on my way home. As I reached an intersection a hedge sprang up, obscuring my vision and I did not see the other car.

- I had been driving for forty years when I fell asleep at the wheel and had an accident.

- I was on the way to the doctor with rear end trouble when my universal joint gave way causing me to have an accident.

- As I approached an intersection a sign suddenly appeared in a place where no stop sign had ever appeared before. I was unable to stop in time to avoid the accident.

- To avoid hitting the bumper of the car in front I struck a pedestrian.

- My car was legally parked as it backed into another vehicle.

cont'd

Reproduced from *50 Ways to Liven Up Your Meetings*, Graham Roberts-Phelps, Gower, Aldershot

- An invisible car came out of nowhere, struck my car and vanished.

- I told the police that I was not injured, but on removing my hat found that I had a fractured skull.

- I was sure the old fellow would never make it to the other side of the road when I struck him.

- The pedestrian had no idea which way to run as I ran over him.

- I saw a slow moving, sad faced old gentleman as he bounced off the roof of my car.

- The indirect cause of the accident was a little guy in a small car with a big mouth.

- I was thrown from my car as it left the road. I was later found in a ditch by some stray cows.

- The telephone pole was approaching. I was attempting to swerve out of the way when I struck the front end.

23   Iceberg chart

Suggested applications
- Data analysis and problem-solving
- Testing learning
- Planning improvements

What happens	Participants work in small groups to brainstorm a specific problem, working within the 'iceberg' principle: that is, that only a small part of any problem is actually visible 'above the water'.
Purpose	To develop a practical approach to solving problems.
Format	Small groups.
Resources	A flipchart. Flipchart paper and pens for each group.
Time	20–45 minutes, or as required.
Introductory notes	'Iceberg' thinking is a useful way of analysing problems and issues. It looks at any situation knowing that many of the issues may not be immediately obvious, or visible. It can be used for a variety of topics, and at any time during a meeting.
Procedure	1. Draw the suggested iceberg illustration (see handout) on a flipchart. Perhaps work through an example by writing a problem or issue in the top part – that is, visible – section of the iceberg and then ask the participants to suggest possible causes or contributing factors which happen beneath the surface. For example, the problem could be due to mistakes being made and the underlying causes may include poor morale, lack of proper systems, no formal quality checks, no written procedures, poor-quality products from suppliers, unrealistic deadlines or no accountability. 2. Either use an issue which you have already identified prior to the meeting or one that has arisen during the meeting.

3. Organize the participants into groups of 4–7, distribute flipchart paper and pens as required, and give them the task of analysing the underlying issues and causes that relate to the problem or situation that you have given them. Allow 15–20 minutes.

4. Ask each group in turn to present back to the main group.

Variations
- Instead of you selecting a problem or issue, ask each group to select a significant problem or difficulty that they face in their work. Once each group has agreed on their topic, ask them to take 15–20 minutes to discuss the issues underlying the problem.
- Instead of giving one issue to all the groups, give different situations or issues to each different group. In this way, a range of different problems or challenges can be addressed.
- Once the underlying causes and issues have been identified, ask everyone to return to their small groups and suggest ways to overcome or prevent some of the underlying causes occurring or to reduce their effect. In this way, the problem or issue can be tackled at source.
- Run a short discussion after each presentation. This discussion should further expand any key terms or phrases in order to firmly establish clear definitions of what the underlying issues or causes might be.

Iceberg chart

A problem is like an iceberg – only part of it is visible above the surface; there are many causes and issues underlying them

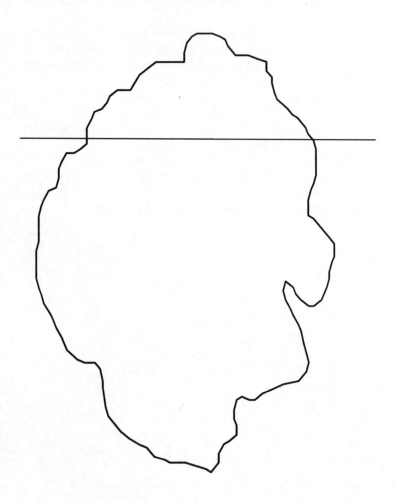

24   Irrelevant facts

This is not so much an activity as such, but rather some useless, irrelevant facts and figures that might make your meeting a little more lively. Perhaps during one of those awkward 'waiting for the coffee to arrive' pauses start a sentence with:

- 'Did you know that ...?'
or
- 'I was reading recently that ... '
or
- Isn't it fascinating to think that ... '

and add one or more of the following 'Useless facts'.

Useless facts

- The longest one-syllable word in the English language is 'screeched'.

- On a Canadian two-dollar bill, the flag flying over the parliament building is an American flag.

- Barbie's measurements, if she were life-sized would be 39–23–33.

- All of the clocks in *Pulp Fiction* are stuck at 4.20.

- No word in the English language rhymes with month.

- A coat hanger is 44 inches long if straightened.

- Canada is an Indian word meaning 'Big Village'.

- 'Dreamt' is the only English word that ends in the letters 'mt'.

- The word 'byte' is a contraction of 'by eight'. The word 'pixel' is a contraction of either 'picture cell' or 'picture element'.

- The average ear of corn has 800 kernels arranged in 16 rows.

- On the new American hundred dollar bill the time on the clock tower of Independence Hall is 4.10.

- Almonds are members of the peach family.

- If you add up the numbers 1 to 100 consecutively (1 + 2 + 3 + 4 + 5 etc.) the total is 5050.

- The term 'the whole nine yards' derives from Second World War fighter pilots in the South Pacific. When arming their airplanes on the ground, the 50 calibre machine-gun ammunition belts measured exactly 27 feet, before being loaded into the fuselage. If the pilots fired all their ammunition at a target, it got 'the whole nine yards'.

- The maximum weight for a golf ball is 1.62 oz.

- The dot over the letter 'i' is called a tittle.

- Mark Twain was born on a day in 1835 when Haley's Comet came into view. When he died in 1910, Haley's Comet came into view again.

- The first hard drive available for the Apple II had a capacity

cont'd

of 5 megabytes.

- In many cases, the amount of storage space on a recordable CD is measured in minutes: 74 minutes is about 650 megabytes; 63 minutes is 550 megabytes.

- Nutmeg is extremely poisonous if injected intravenously.

- Only one-third of the people who can twitch their ears can twitch only one at a time.

- Winston Churchill was born in a ladies' room during a dance.

- The most common name in the world is Mohammed.

- The word 'set' has more definitions than any other word in the English language.

- There were four consecutive full moons making two blue moons in 1999 (2 and 31 January and 2 and 3 March). The only other time this happened during the twentieth century was in 1915 (1 and 31 January and 1 and 31 March).

- 'Underground' is the only word in the English language that begins and ends with the letters 'und'.

- A full 7 per cent of the entire Irish barley crop goes into the production of Guinness beer.

- If you toss a penny 10 000 times, it will not be heads 5000 times, but more like 4950 – the heads picture weighs more, so it more frequently ends at the bottom.

- Einstein couldn't speak fluently when he was nine. His parents thought he might be retarded.

- In Los Angeles, there are fewer people than there are cars.

- You are more likely to be stung by a bee on a windy day than in any other weather.

- The average person laughs about 15 times a day.

- Research indicates that mosquitoes are attracted to people who have recently eaten bananas.

- Penguins can jump as high as six feet in the air.

- The average person is about a quarter of an inch taller at night.

- A sneeze zooms out of your mouth at over 600 mph.

cont'd

- Neanderthal man's brain was bigger than yours is.
- *Donald Duck* comics were banned from Finland because he doesn't wear pants.
- Your right lung takes in more air than your left one.
- Women's hearts beat faster than men's.
- Pollsters say that 40 per cent of dog and cat owners carry pictures of the pets in their wallets.
- You can only smell 1/20th as well as a dog.
- The world population of chickens is about equal to the number of people.
- It is estimated that there are as many rats in the UK as people – over 50 million!
- Every time Beethoven sat down to write music, he poured iced water over his head.
- A monkey was once tried and convicted for smoking a cigarette in South Bend, Indiana.
- Some toothpastes contain antifreeze.
- Sigmund Freud had a morbid fear of ferns.
- Bird droppings are the chief export of Nauru, an island nation in the Western Pacific.
- There are more plastic flamingos in America than real ones.
- Mosquitoes have teeth.
- Spotted skunks do handstands before they spray.
- The best-known Western names in China are Jesus Christ, Richard Nixon and Elvis Presley.
- Most cows give more milk when they listen to music.
- In 1980 a Las Vegas hospital suspended workers for betting on when patients would die.
- Thomas Edison was afraid of the dark. (Hence, the light bulb?)

25 Lateral thinking

Suggested applications
- Ice-breaker
- Energizer
- Encouraging creativity

What happens

Participants work in small groups or pairs to find a solution to a given puzzle or problem.

Purpose

To get participants working in pairs or small groups and to practise creativity or lateral thinking.

Format

Pairs/small groups.

Resources

A copy of the handout for each pair or small group.

Time

10–15 minutes, or as required.

Procedure

1. Introduce the activity by explaining that lateral thinking is about thinking outside of normal 'straight-line' thinking. It requires the ability to change viewpoints, examine the non-obvious, and often generate ideas from the intuitive, creative or subconscious part of our minds. However, once discovered, a 'lateral' solution is often a 'blinding flash of the obvious'.
2. Organize the participants in pairs or small groups.
3. Allocate one puzzle or problem to each pair or group (see handout). You may either choose to use the same one for each group or different problems for different groups.
4. Tell the participants to take no more than 10 minutes (or however long you choose) to suggest possible answers.
5. Encourage the participants to think 'laterally' and concentrate on generating a large number of ideas, allowing one thought to flow into another.
6. Ask the group or pairs for their solutions and give out the suggested answers.

Lateral thinking puzzles

Fizzy puzzle

A man had a jug full of lemonade and a jug full of milk. He poured them both into one large jug. Yet he kept the two liquids separate. How?

Speeding ticket

A woman is driving her smart new car at ten miles per hour down a quiet sidestreet in her neighbourhood. A traffic policeman spots her, stops the car and fines the woman on the spot for speeding. Why?

Call box

A woman depended on a telephone box at the end of her road to make calls, but it was often out of order. Each day she reported the problem to the telephone company, but nothing was done. Finally, in desperation, she phoned the company with a false piece of information which caused the telephone to be fixed within hours. What did she tell them?

Catching a bullet

A man fires a bullet and another man catches the bullet with his bare hands. The bullet does not touch anything – except the air, of course – from the gun to the hand. The second man is uninjured. How does he do it? (There are two solutions – can you find them both?)

Reproduced from *50 Ways to Liven Up Your Meetings*, Graham Roberts-Phelps, Gower, Aldershot

Lateral thinking puzzles: answers

Fizzy puzzle

> A: They were both frozen as ice cubes.

Speeding ticket

> A: In the early days of motoring, the speed limit was eight miles per hour.

Call box

> A: She told them that, due to a fault it was possible to make free international calls from the box and the telephone was very busy as a result!

Catching a bullet

> A: The first man fires the bullet vertically up a cliff face and the second man is standing on the top of the cliff. The other answer is the man fires the bullet from the back of a jet plane travelling at the same speed as the bullet, but in the opposite direction. The bullet, according to the laws of physics, would fall to the ground as it has no horizontal velocity.

Reproduced from *50 Ways to Liven Up Your Meetings*, Graham Roberts-Phelps, Gower, Aldershot

26 Mental power

Suggested applications
- Ice-breaker
- Energizer
- Encouraging creativity
- Data analysis and problem-solving

What happens
Participants work individually to complete the mental challenge which they are given. The entire group then reviews how easy or difficult they found the question.

Purpose
To practise mental agility and improve concentration.

Format
Individual/main group discussion.

Resources
None.

Time
5–10 minutes, or as required.

Procedure
1. Introduce the activity by saying that, in this modern age of calculators, computers and digital toys, our brains have less to do in many respects. Explain that this simple exercise reawakens some of the natural skills and agility that we developed during our education but perhaps use less frequently now.
2. Read out the following instruction to the participants:

   'In your head, count the number of capital letters in the alphabet that contain curved lines.'

3. Ask them to write the answer down when they have it.
4. Wait until everybody, or nearly everybody, has finished the exercise before asking for, and checking their answers. (The correct answer is 11.)
5. Run a brief discussion using the following 'Discussion points'.

Discussion points
- How far did you get?
- What techniques did you use? Visualization?
- How hard was it to concentrate?
- How can you learn better concentration skills?

27 Mind Map®*

Suggested applications
- Encouraging group-working
- Building rapport
- Encouraging creativity

What happens Participants work in small groups or pairs to practise the technique of mind-mapping.

Purpose To map existing views and knowledge at the start of a meeting or to examine issues or summarize problems at the end of the session.

Format Small groups/pairs.

Resources A Flipchart.
Flipchart paper and multi-coloured pens for each pair or small group.

Time 15–20 minutes, or as required, plus group review.

Introductory notes Mind-mapping is a way of notating ideas or thoughts that is markedly different from using logical or lateral thinking. Instead of listing things in a sequence, typically from the top to the bottom of a page, mind-mapping allows ideas to literally flow in a lateral or completely non-logical sequence around the page.

A Mind Map can also incorporate such things as pictures, icons and different colours to denote different meanings or themes. For example, if you are mind-mapping a topic such as Hollywood you would write the word 'Hollywood' in the middle, of a page then allow your thoughts to develop to, say, Clint Eastwood, then to 'spaghetti' because of 'Spaghetti Westerns, and drawing a branch off showing a plateful of spaghetti.

* A concept created by Tony Buzan

116

As bizarre as this may sound, research and experiments have shown that using mind-mapping can aid recall and comprehension.

Procedure
1. Draw an example Mind Map on a flipchart in advance, remembering that it might contain different colours, pictures and icons.
2. Introduce the activity by reviewing the elements of a Mind Map and the rationale behind it – that is, it allows lateral thinking and the free flow of ideas.
3. Select an issue related to the meeting and organize the participants into small groups or pairs to produce a Mind Map depicting that issue. Provide flipchart paper and multi-coloured pens, and allow them 15–20 minutes to complete the task.
4. Display the flipchart pages around the room, and ask everyone to circulate and to review the maps.

Variations
- Introduce the concept of mind-mapping right at the start of your meeting and then at regular intervals, – say, once an hour. Direct the participants to return to their Mind Maps and add additional elements to summarize the points or ideas that have just been covered. In this way the Mind Map will actually build up into an effective and memorable summary of the meeting and its outcomes.
- At the end of the activity allow more time for the participants to fine-tune their Mind Map before displaying it and presenting the best to the whole group.
- When the pairs or groups have been working on their Mind Maps for five minutes, stop them and rotate their positions, leaving the Mind Maps on which they are working in place. Each group or pair will then continue working on somebody else's Mind Map. In this way, certain words and ideas might cross-fertilize.

Mind Map

Draw a mind map, letting your
ideas flow as they come to you

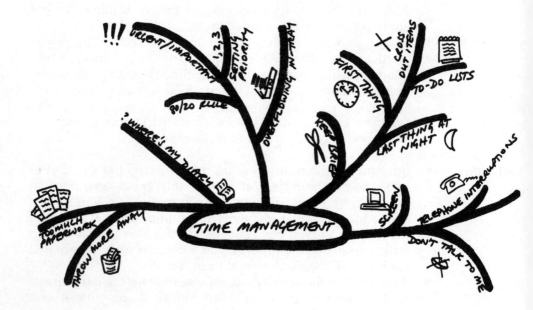

28 Mind reading

Suggested applications
- Ice-breaker
- Building rapport

What happens You use quick mental arithmetic to create an illusion of mind-reading.

Purpose To sharpen thinking and get participants working together.

Format Pairs/Individual.

Resources None.

Time 10–15 minutes, or as required.

Procedure **Note:** Read 'How to do it' before attempting to follow the instructions below.

1. Ask a participant to jot down on a scrap of paper any three-figure number, over 300, that comes into their head, while you do the same. Neither of you must see what the other is writing.
2. When you have both done this, take a separate piece of paper, gaze intently at the participant's forehead, scribble down another number quickly and fold the paper up small. Explain that you have been trying to see into his mind, and ask him to take charge of the folded-up paper without looking at it.
3. Now tell them the three-figure number that you wrote down on the first piece of paper, and which you still have, and ask them to add it to their own.
4. Ask:

   - 'Is the result a four-figure number? Yes? Well, put a ring round the last three figures.'

- 'Is the ringed number lower than the number you chose? Then subtract it from your number and write down the result.'
- 'Now what you've done is to subtract one number that I don't know from another that I don't know. Obviously I can't tell you the answer. I shall have to get you to tell me. What was it? 158?'

5. The participant then unfolds the paper you put in his charge. Amazingly, the number you scribbled down was 158!

How to do it This feat appears incredibly difficult, although it is very easy indeed. You already know that the answer will be 158 before you even start the trick.

The number which you gave the participant to add to their own was 842. The number which you wrote down on the folded piece of paper was 158 which is the result of 842 subtracted from 1000. No matter what number he chooses himself, the final answer will be 158.

You can alter the answer each time you do the trick. Always choose a three-figure number over 700 for your first number. Then secretly, subtract that number from 1000 and write the resulting figure on the folded piece of paper which you put in the participants charge. For example, if your chosen number is 793, the concealed number which you give the participant, and the final answer, will be 207.

Don't do this trick more than a couple of times at once. Try to leave your audience rather puzzled and wanting a little more.

29   Minute talk

Suggested applications
- Ice-breaker
- Energizer

What happens
One or more volunteers present a topic spontaneously for one minute in front of the group.

Purpose
To act as an entertaining ice-breaker to mark the start or end of a topic or create a necessary diversion. Also useful for practising presentation skills or for highlighting certain themes of selected topics.

Format
Group.

Resources
A flipchart and marker pens.

Time
10–15 minutes, or as required.

Introductory notes
Many people fear speaking in front of an audience. This activity allows the opportunity to stand up in front of a group and improvise without having to know, remember or prove anything. It's an effective way to help them feel relaxed in front of a group. You can begin by setting a 30-second time limit and increase this as the participants become more comfortable with the format. Not everyone needs to play every game. Just two or three minutes (that is, two or three people playing) will be sufficient to energize the meeting.

Procedure
1. First, find a volunteer. Say to the group, 'I need a volunteer for a One-Minute Talk. Are there any risk-takers? ... Great ... We're going to find a subject for you to discuss. Who has an idea?'
2. Next ask the group to suggest a number of topics – for example, the weather, sunburn, washing dishes, skateboarding – and write them up on the flipchart.

Alternatively, choose topics relevant to your meeting theme.
3. Ask the volunteer to choose one of these topics.
4. Tell the volunteer that they have one minute to talk about their topic without stopping, except to take a breath. If they run out of things to say, they should make something up, but try not to stray from the subject.
5. Ask for another volunteer and repeat the process until the group is visibly energized and more alert.

Variations
*   Once people feel comfortable with this game, you can add another dimension to it. Slowly increase the amount of time for the people until they can create a complete story – on the spot.
*   You also can use an object such as a cane or wand or table-tennis bat as a 'talking stick'. The participant holding the talking stick creates a story. When they have finished speaking, they hand the talking stick to another person who continues the story. Each person embellishes or moves the story forwards.

30 Morning train

Suggested applications
- Ice-breaker
- Building rapport

What happens   Participants try to sort out their morning papers on an imaginary train.

Purpose   To provide a humorous diversion or act as an ice-breaker.

Format   Individual.

Resources   For each participant: a chair plus a newspaper with the pages mixed up.

Time   5–10 minutes, or as required.

Procedure
1. First, arrange two rows of chairs, one for each participant, placed facing each other. These chairs represent the train.
2. Ask the participants to be seated on the chairs and give each 'passenger' a newspaper whose pages have been thoroughly mixed up beforehand. On your signal to start all the passengers begin to put their newspapers straight – pages the right way up and in the right order.
3. The winner is the participant who is first to put their newspaper right, but usually there isn't any winner; a crowded train is more likely to result in a torn, rather than a tidy, newspaper!

31   My secret

Suggested applications
- Ice-breaker
- Building rapport

What happens   Each participant writes down a little-known fact or interesting anecdote about themselves. Once the papers are collected in, the group has to try to guess the owner of each 'secret'.

Purpose   To break the ice at the beginning of a meeting, particularly if the participants already know each other. Also, to encourage the sharing of information in an informal, lighthearted and non-threatening manner and to help team-building.

Format   Individual/main group discussion.

Resources   A flipchart and marker pens.

Time   10–15 minutes, or as required.

Procedure   1. Ask the participants to write down on a piece of paper something that nobody else in the room knows about them. (Perhaps include one yourself.)
2. Collect all the papers and shuffle them. One at a time, read out the secret and write one word to summarize it on the flipchart.
3. Ask the rest of the group to try to guess who is the owner of the 'secret'.
4. When guessed correctly, write the name of the owner of the 'secret' against each.
5. Continue until the owners of all the 'secrets' are revealed.
6. Run a group discussion.

Discussion points
- How did you feel about colleagues correctly or incorrectly attributing a 'secret' to you?

- Does knowing the 'secret' change your perspective of anybody?

Variations
- Try including one or two red herrings that do not belong to anybody just to try to get people thinking.
- Give the activity a different focus by asking participants to write down a secret, but maybe embarrassing, moment or to confess something they have done in the past and got away with it (of a minor nature hopefully!).
- Ask the group to write down a phrase or expression that was used to describe them in a school report.

32 Number jumble

Suggested applications
- Ice-breaker
- Focusing individuals

What happens Participants take part in a simple exercise to find out how good they are at remembering things.

Purpose To explore the capacity for memory and juggling numbers.

Format Small groups.

Resources An OHP or a copy of the handout for each participant.

Time 5–10 minutes, or as required.

Introductory notes Most people can juggle five numbers in their heads with relative ease. Seven numbers becomes fairly difficult and 14 numbers seems to be impossible. Psychologists suggest that most of us can carry, at most, about seven discrete bits of information at a time. In other words, we can deal fairly easily with a seven-digit telephone number, with seven countries in a continent and with seven new people in a meeting. Any more than that and we need either to write things down or to rearrange the information in a more manageable way.

Procedure
1. Before the meeting make up an OHP slide of the handout on page 128.
2. First, organize the participants into groups of about 4.
3. Introduce the activity by saying that studies have shown that there are definite limits to our attention span. We can concentrate only so long on something before our mind skips on to something else. Another limitation is that we can juggle only so many items in our minds at any one time.
4. To demonstrate this, ask the participants to try the following exercise: 'Read each of the following series of numbers to

yourself. After each series, close your eyes, and repeat the numbers or write them down. Which is the longest series you can hold in your mind?'

5. Display the OHP slide to the group, revealing one line of numbers at a time.

6. When all the numbers have been attempted, reveal each line again, asking the participants to score two points for each correct number in the correct sequence, and one point for the correct number out of sequence.

Variation   Distribute a copy of the handout to each participant and ask them to follow the instructions. Then score as per step 6 above.

Number jumble

Read each of the following series of numbers to yourself. After each series, close your eyes, and repeat the numbers or write them down.

Which is the longest series you can hold in your mind?

3 5 4 8 4

5 7 9 1 3 2

2 5 4 7 7 0 4

8 5 7 1 3 2 7 0

2 4 6 5 8 4 2 4 5

1 2 6 1 9 4 1 7 2 1 1 9 6 9

33 Parking lot

Suggested applications
- Practising group-working
- Data analysis and problem-solving
- Planning improvements
- Controlling the meeting

What happens
During a meeting, whenever items or points are raised that you would like to delay, deflect or defer, park them on the parking lot.

Purpose
To gather together any issues questions, observations, concerns and so on about the subject under discussion or related topics for later review, thus minimizing interruptions and unnecessary deflections from the purpose of the meeting.

Format
Individual/main group discussion.

Resources
A pre-drawn flipchart page.

Time
As required.

Introductory notes
In any meeting, issues can be raised which are outside the scope of either the chairperson's jurisdiction or the content of the meeting. These may be issues that are specific to an individual's relationship with their manager or perhaps to do with the organization's policies or procedures or, even politics.

This mechanism prevents such issues interrupting the meeting or impacting on the chairperson's credibility in handling them by capturing them positively and allowing the meeting to move on to focus on the matters in hand.

Procedure
1. This mechanism is best set up and described within the first few minutes of the meeting, perhaps when you are running through the logistics and meeting timing. Take a piece of flipchart paper and divide it into a parking lot. Review and

summarise at the end of the meeting or at some point following it.

2. Draw the illustration on the following page on a flipchart page.
3. Post the page at the side or back of the room, or perhaps next to the coffee station.
4. Give each participant a Post-it notepad.
5. Explain that if they have any points that come to mind on any aspect of the meeting content to write them on a Post-it note and stick it on the parking lot during an appropriate break.
6. Review the Post-its at regular intervals during the day.

Variations
- Your review session can discuss each of the Post-its on the parking lot and group them together, perhaps rewording them into two or three clear issues that are being missed.
- Following the meeting, write a short note to the participants referring back to the issues on the parking lot and explaining your procedure in dealing with them.
- If the meeting is part of an ongoing series, review the process of dealing with these issues at a subsequent meeting.

Parking lot

Please park your issues, questions, concerns or queries here.

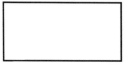

34   Pass the compliment

Suggested applications
- Ice-breaker
- Building rapport
- Encouraging communication

What happens   Each participant whispers to another participant a one-word compliment. The recipient then adds another complimentary word and passes the compliment on to another. The process is continued, adding a complimentary word each time to the final participant who repeats the entire compliment out loud.

Purpose   To improve rapport and get participants working together.

Format   Main group.

Resources   None.

Time   10–15 minutes, or as required.

Introductory notes   Can you imagine what would happen if, in future, all gatherings conducted by the United Nations started out with three compliments given to each nation attending? It's a little hard to imagine, which is why this exercise was created.

Based on the old 'Pass the Whisper' game, this activity is fun and energizing, while slipping in soothing strokes that will act as a salve. It is particularly suitable for conferences and large meetings that last at least one day.

Procedure   1.   Say to the participants: 'How many of you remember playing the game "Pass the Whisper"? It is also called the "Telephone Game". Well, for those of you who aren't sure, it is a listening game. We are going to play a special version of it today called "Pass the Compliment".'

'I want you to think of a complimentary word that you would like to give to the person behind you. Use a word that compliments the person's character, such as "friendly", "clever", or "kind", rather than one that compliments the person's appearance, such as "slim", "handsome", or "attractive". If you don't know the person behind you, imagine that you are giving the person a compliment as a gift. Wouldn't it be great if we could give people a positive quality just by whispering it in their ears? Well, who's to say we can't?'

'Does everybody have a word? We are going to do this by rows. We'll start with the front row. Please turn to the person behind you and whisper, "I want you to know that I think that you are ...". For example, you might use the word "incredible". Then whisper your compliment. That person will whisper to the person behind them "I want you to know that I think that you are 'incredible' and 'fabulous' ". The third person must remember the first two compliments and add a third, and so on all the way through the rows. The final person must say the entire complimentary sentence aloud!'

2. Have each row check that each person repeats the compliments correctly.

Variations
- Pick one participant at the end of each day and have each of their colleagues give that person a compliment.
- Take a compliment break in which people give group compliments randomly, such as, 'We're great teamworkers!' or 'We're good and getting better all the time!'.
- Start an 'I'm great because ...' sheet of paper and post it around the room. When the last person has added their comment, read the entire list back to the meeting.
- Instead of compliments, have a person in the first row make a funny face. When the first person has made a face that they can maintain, they turn around and show it to the person sitting behind. Encourage people not to laugh or lose their concentration. The individual who is passing the 'funny face' holds the pose until the person who is receiving the face can imitate it. Once the second person has mirrored the first person's funny face as closely as possible, that person makes a different facial expression, turns around and passes the new face to the next person. This continues until everyone has had a chance to imitate a face and make up a new one. This variation, will generate a great deal of laughter.

35   Pirate raid

Suggested applications
- Practising group-working
- Building rapport
- Ice-breaker

What happens

Participants work in two or more teams to 'scavenge' for a list of items or information.

Purpose

To test participants' influencing, creativity and lateral thinking skills and to promote team working.

Format

Small groups.

Resources

One copy of each handout. Small prizes for the winning team.

Time

20–25 minutes, or as required.

Introductory notes

This activity asks participants to 'raid' and 'plunder' the office or venue, or nearby shops and so on, to obtain a list of items. It doesn't matter if some of the items are unobtainable, or cannot be obtained in the time limit: this is part of the fun. This activity, if run at the beginning of a meeting, will get participants working together. It is also a good warm-up and ice-breaking activity, particularly for longer meetings.

Procedure

1. Organize the participants into two teams and distribute handouts A and B – one to each team.
2. Tell the two teams that they are to gather as many of the items listed within the time limit. Tell them also the area in which they may search.
3. Allow 15–20 minutes for the 'pirate raid' and a further 5–10 minutes to see which team has won, and to discuss how various items were obtained. (Make sure that any 'borrowed' items are returned!)
4. Award small prizes, such as chocolate bars, to the participants in the winning team.

Pirate raid A

As a test of your powers of persuasion, creativity and lateral-thinking, collect as many of the items listed within the time limit given. One point will be awarded for every item collected, and one bonus point for every minute under the time limit, but only if all items are collected.

- some foreign currency

- a cheque for £1 000 000

- a boiled sweet

- the name and address of a complete stranger (in their handwriting)

- a piece of underwear

- a cooking utensil

- the price of a Ford Escort

- a car number plate

- a toilet roll

- a coin dated before 1980

- a £50 note

- the telephone number of the British Embassy in Paris

- the full name and date of birth of your managing director

Reproduced from *50 Ways to Liven Up Your Meetings*, Graham Roberts-Phelps, Gower, Aldershot

Pirate raid B

As a test of your powers of persuasion, creativity and lateral-thinking, collect as many of the items listed within the time limit given. One point will be awarded for every item collected, and one bonus point for every minute under the time limit, but only if all items are collected.

- some foreign currency

- a cheque for £1 000 000

- a piece of fruit

- the name and address of a complete stranger (in their handwriting)

- a flower

- a workshop tool

- the price of a dozen eggs

- a sign or notice

- a very old newspaper or magazine

- a coin dated before 1980

- a £50 note

- the telephone number of the French Embassy in London

- the full name and date of birth of your youngest employee

Reproduced from *50 Ways to Liven Up Your Meetings*, Graham Roberts-Phelps, Gower, Aldershot

36   Puzzle phrases

Suggested applications
- Ice-breaker
- Encouraging creativity

What happens   Participants try to guess the answer to this popular form of brain-teaser.

Purpose   To encourage creativity and to introduce a change of pace.

Format   Main group discussion.

Resources   An OHP or flipchart.

Time   10–15 minutes, or as required.

Introductory notes   This type of brain-teaser has proven to be a popular ice-breaker and can be used as an intriguing and light-hearted way of starting or finishing any meeting.

The collection of puzzles that follows has been selected because of the ease with which they can be drawn onto a flipchart or OHP slide. You can use them formally by putting up four or five at a time, or simply use one between sessions or different topics.

Procedure
1. Draw one or more 'Puzzles phrases' (see pages 139–47) on to a flipchart page or OHP slide.
2. Invite participants to guess a well-known phrase or saying that each might represent.
3. Use 'Puzzle phrase: example' for demonstration purposes, if needed.

Note: Answers are given on page 148.

Variations
- As a variation, after running the exercise once or twice during a meeting, task participants with designing or

creating their own puzzles for the rest of the group to guess.

- Start off with some of the easier puzzles and work through to some of the more difficult ones, leaving these open from one meeting to another, giving the participants more time to solve them.

Puzzle phrase: example

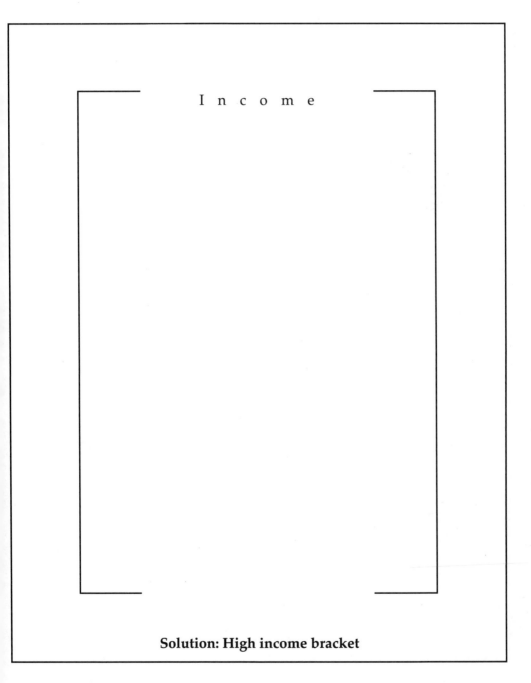

I n c o m e

Solution: High income bracket

Puzzle phrases 1

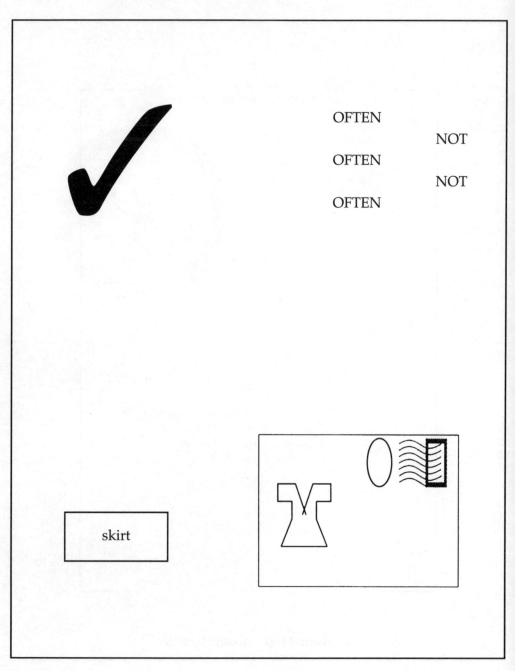

OFTEN

                   NOT

OFTEN

                   NOT

OFTEN

skirt

Puzzle phrases 2

Puzzle phrases 3

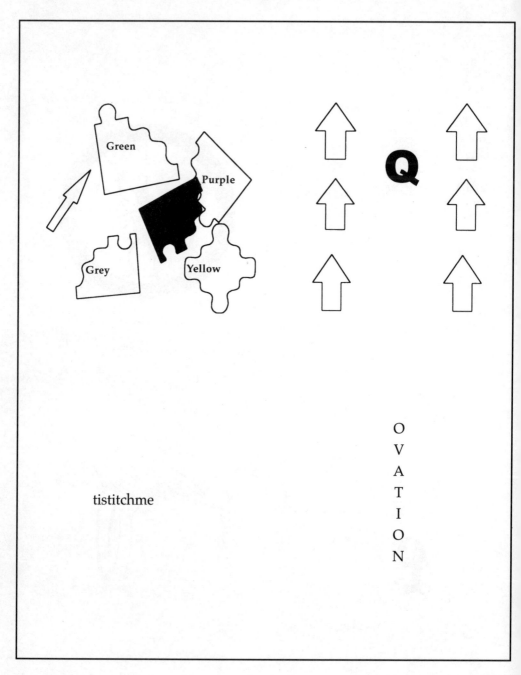

Puzzle phrases 4

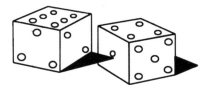

L NCH
L NCH

VA DERS

$$\frac{NO\ \ NO}{CORRECT}$$

Puzzle phrases 5

Puzzle phrases 6

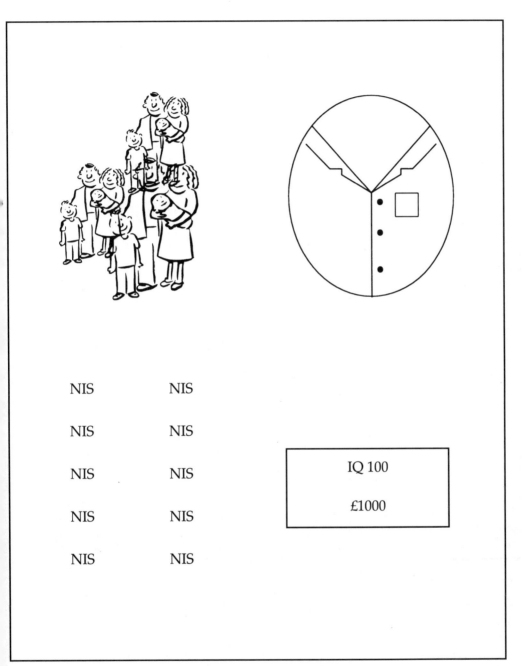

Puzzle phrases 7

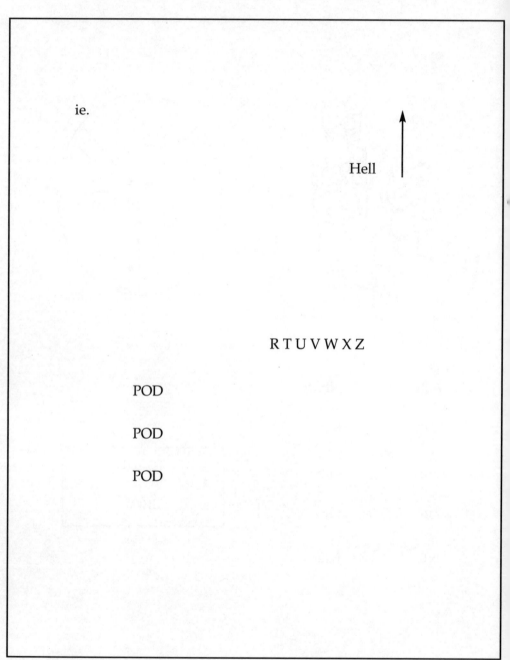

ie.

Hell ↑

R T U V W X Z

POD

POD

POD

Puzzle phrases 8

12:30   S U I T

12:30

(O R)

(I G)   S L I P

              N O !

Reproduced from *50 Ways to Liven Up Your Meetings*, Graham Roberts-Phelps, Gower, Aldershot

Solutions to puzzle phrases

Puzzle phrase 1

- Just a tick
- More often than not
- Mini skirt
- Address

Puzzle phrase 5

- Mixed doubles
- Last but not least
- Weather cock
- Jail birds

Puzzle phrase 2

- Banana split
- Spokesman
- Money talks
- Time flies

Puzzle phrase 6

- Happy families
- Jacket potato
- Tennis
- More money than sense

Puzzle phrase 3

- Greenpeace
- Queue up
- A stitch in time
- Standing ovation

Puzzle phrase 7

- That is beside the point
- Hello (Hell-low)
- Tripod
- Nosy (No 's' or 'y')

Puzzle phrase 4

- Paradise
- Take you out to lunch
- Space invaders
- Right under your nose

Puzzle phrase 8

- Time and time again
- Space suit
- Originate
- Slip knot

37   Quotation quiz

Suggested applications
- Practising group-working
- Ice-breaker
- Building rapport
- Focusing individuals

What happens   Participants try to match quotations with their originators.

Purpose   To build rapport and focus concentration.

Format   Individual/pairs/small groups/main group discussion.

Resources   An OHP or flipchart or copies of the handout, as appropriate.

Time   10–15 minutes or as required.

Introductory notes   This activity can be adapted to any type of format and is an unusual way of either starting or ending a meeting.

The collection of quotations that follows appeals to me and suits my training courses, but, if you prefer, it should be easy to create your own quiz sheets.

Procedure
1. Depending on the format you decide to use, either distribute copies of the selected handout(s) or read out loud or write one or more quotations on to a flipchart.
2. Invite the participants to guess who said the quotation, some of which are quite well known. Encourage them to guess those that they don't know.

Note: Answers are given on page 153.

Variations
- After running the exercise once or twice during a meeting, task participants with designing or creating their own puzzles for the rest of the group to guess.
- Ask the participants to invent some of their own to test the group.

Quotation quiz 1

Decide which of the following, rather rude, quotations are attributed to which famous individuals:

Oscar Wilde, Groucho Marx, Alan Bennett, Groucho Marx, Robert Redford, Billy Wilder, Jackie Mason, Joseph Heller (*Catch-22*), Mark Twain, Winston Churchill

	Quotation	Person
1.	Britain is the only country in the world where the food is more dangerous than the sex.	
2.	Americans always try to do the right thing – after they've tried everything else.	
3.	Don't look now, but there's one too many in this room and I think it's you,	
4.	Don't point that beard at me, it might go off.	
5.	Only dull people are brilliant at breakfast.	
6.	I didn't attend the funeral, but I sent a nice letter saying I approved of it.	
7.	He has the attention span of a lightning bolt.	
8.	He has Van Gogh's ear for music.	
9.	So boring you fall asleep halfway through her name.	
10.	Some men are born mediocre, some men achieve mediocrity, and some men have mediocrity thrust upon them.	

Quotation quiz 2

Decide which of the following quotations are attributed to which famous individuals:

Henry T. Ford, Cicero, Galileo, Thomas A. Edison, Albert Einstein, Napoleon, Oscar Wilde, Mark Twain, Peter F. Drucker, William Shakespeare, Oliver Wendell Holmes

Quotation	Person
1. There is nothing so useless as doing efficiently that which should not be done at all.	
2. The old believe everything; the middle-aged suspect everything; the young know everything.	
3. It is better to deserve honours and not have them than to have them and not deserve them.	
4. We are such stuff As dreams are made of, And our little life Is rounded with a sleep.	
5. It's faith in something and enthusiasm for something that makes life worth living.	
6. Victory belongs to the most persevering.	
7. Try not to become a man of success but rather try to become a man of value.	
8. The three great essentials to achieve anything worth while are first, hard work; second, stick-to-it-iveness; third, common sense.	
9. Whether you believe you can, or whether you believe you can't – you're right!	

cont'd

Reproduced from *50 Ways to Liven Up Your Meetings*, Graham Roberts-Phelps, Gower, Aldershot

Quotation	Person
10. Learning is a kind of natural food for the mind.	
11. You cannot teach a man anything; you can only help him to find it within himself.	

Quotation quiz: answers

Quotation quiz 1

1. Jackie Mason
2. Winston Churchill
3. Groucho Marx
4. Groucho Marx
5. Oscar Wilde
6. Mark Twain
7. Robert Redford
8. Billy Wilder
9. Alan Bennett
10. Joseph Heller (*Catch-22*)

Quotation quiz 2

1. Peter F. Drucker
2. Oscar Wilde
3. Mark Twain
4. William Shakespeare
5. Oliver Wendell Holmes
6. Napoleon
7. Albert Einstein
8. Thomas A. Edison
9. Henry T. Ford
10. Cicero
11. Galileo

38   Reactive debate

Suggested applications
- Practising group-working
- Data analysis and problem-solving
- Planning improvements

What happens   Participants work in an unusual way to discuss one or more issues in a 'debating forum'.

Purpose   To sharpen thinking and get participants working in pairs or small groups.

Format   Pairs/small groups.

Resources   None.

Time   20–25 minutes, or as required.

Introductory notes   A good debate is a great way to stimulate the mind and to get the blood flowing! This activity will bring a whole new world of ideas and perspectives into the meeting. Especially suited to meetings that require a variety of perspectives.

Procedure
1. Explain to the participants that they are going to approach the discussion in a unique way. Ask between 6–10 people to bring their chairs up to the front of the room. Divide them into two rows facing each other. Label as 'Team A' and 'Team B'.
2. Explain that the two rows are going to debate a motion on a 'for or against' basis. Team A will be 'for' the issue and Team B will be 'against' it.
3. Now explain that this will not just be an ordinary debate. Each participant must choose a character from the past, present or future who supports the position that they are taking – either for or against the issue – and will become this character for the sake of lively discussion. Emphasize that it

is OK if the participants do not agree with the side that they are given and, in fact, this is all the better, because it will help them see it from a different perspective. If they wish, they can take on the posture or voice of their chosen character as well as represent their perspective on the issue under discussion.

4. Give the teams a few minutes to decide upon their characters, then ask each participant to introduce themselves as their character, to the rest of the group.

5. Announce the motion or topic of debate. Try to avoid obvious or very controversial issues and, instead, pick topical examples or one that is related to the theme of the meeting or event.

6. Remind the participants that they will respond to any questions asked 'in the spirit of their chosen character'. After about 10 minutes of discussion between Teams A and B, the rest of the group can ask questions of either team, or of a particular character.

Variation   Instead of letting participants select their own characters, write the names of characters on 3 x 5 cards and give them out at random.

39   Sequential

Suggested applications
- Ice-breaker
- Data analysis and problem-solving

What happens   Participants work individually to identify the next word in a sequence.

Purpose   To help sharpen thinking.

Format   Individual.

Resources   A copy of the handout for each participant.
An OHP (optional).

Time   10–15 minutes, or as required.

Procedure   1.   Distribute a copy of the handout to each participant or display it as an OHP slide.
2.   Give the participants 5 minutes to work individually on the task.
3.   When the time is up, go around the room asking the participants to say what they think they have found.
4.   Run a brief discussion using the 'discussion points' below.

The answer   ONEROUS. The others end in the numbers ten, nine and eight respectively. 'Onerous contains the number 'one' but this is not in sequence with the others. It also appears at the beginning of the word rather than at the end.

Discussion points
- Did you find it easy or difficult to think of the answer?
- Why do you think you found the problem easy/difficult to solve?

Sequential thinking

Often

Onerous

Canine

Freight

Which word is not in sequence with the others?

40   Short roads

Suggested applications
- Ice-breaker
- Energizer
- Encouraging creativity
- Data analysis and problem-solving

What happens   Participants work in pairs to ask question about, and then guess the answer to, a puzzle.

Purpose   To practise creative and lateral thinking.

Format   Pairs.

Resources   A copy of the handout for each pair.

Time   10–15 minutes, or as required.

Procedure   1. Ask the participants to work in pairs on this exercise, which will test their lateral thinking ability and creativity.
2. Either distribute a copy of the handout to each pair, read the story out loud or display it as an OHP. Allow the participants 10–15 minutes to solve the problem.
3. You might choose to provide short 'yes' or 'no' answers to participants' questions, although be careful not to lead them too quickly to the answer. Encourage them to explore all possible options, thinking as laterally and creatively as possible.
4. When the time is up, ask each pair to read out their answers or conclusion.

The answer   It is difficult to believe that a solution exists that requires less road than solution no. 3, but the Minister was quite correct. There *is* a solution which links all four towns with less total road. There are no tricks or corny catches involved.

   The shortest distance is shown below. It represents 27.3 miles of road and therefore saves a mile in road-building expense compared to the two diagonals. Someone starting from A would have a shorter journey to D, but a larger journey to B or C.

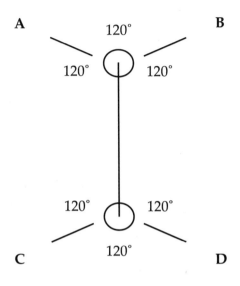

Variation   Ask the participants to work on the problem in small groups, in order to create more of a group interaction and team-building exercise.

Short roads

There are four main towns in Squareville. We will call them A, B, C and D. They lie at the corners of a 10-mile square. In order to improve communications between the towns, the Squareville Department of Transport decided to build a new road linking all four towns together. Because they had very little money, it was decided that the new road system should be as short as possible and still allow access from any one town or another. The engineers came up with three designs, shown below.

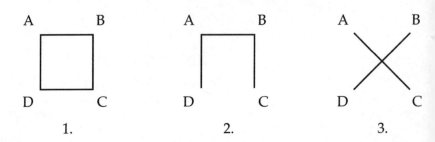

Solution no. 1 uses 40 miles of road, no. 2 uses 30 miles of road and no. 3 uses 28.3 miles of road. The designers naturally recommended plan three, because it employed the smallest road area, and therefore cost the least. When they showed the plans to the Minister of Finance, he accused them of extravagance and pointed out an even better design which had even less road surface.

What was it?

Reproduced from *50 Ways to Liven Up Your Meetings*, Graham Roberts-Phelps, Gower, Aldershot

41   Spelling bee

Suggested applications
- Ice-breaker
- Energizer
- Building rapport
- Practising group-working

What happens   Participants work in small groups to test each other's spelling skills.

Purpose   To sharpen thinking and get participants working in pairs or small groups.

Format   Small groups.

Resources   A copy of the handout for each group.

Time   10–15 minutes, or as required.

Procedure
1. Organize the participants into small groups of 4–6, with one person taking the role of 'spelling master'.
2. Distribute a copy of the handout to each group.
3. Within each group, the spelling master asks each person, in turn, to spell one word – and a point is scored if the word is spelt right. If the participant fails to spell the word correctly the same word should not be passed on to the next person, for the task of spelling it would, of course, be easier after hearing the predecessor's error.
4. End the activity by asking the participants to nominate their 'champion speller'.

Variation   An alternative method is to give everyone a pencil and some paper. Each participant then writes down every word as it is announced. At the end each participant passes their paper to their neighbour for marking. The words are then spelt out in turn and all those which are written correctly are ticked.

Spelling bee

Instructions for the 'Spelling master'

- Ask each person, in turn, to spell one word from the list below. Award one point if the word is spelt correctly.

Note: If someone fails to spell a word correctly, do not pass on the same word to the next person, because the task of spelling it would be easier after hearing their predecessor's error.

Aboriginal	Accommodation	Applause
Appreciable	Beautiful	Bradawl
Catastrophe	Cellular	Contemporaneous
Crystal	Debility	Embarrassment
Emphasis	Endeavour	Forty
Grammar	Grandeur	Holocaust
Knead	Laboratory	Loveable
Marvellous	Mitre	Morale
Necessary	Neurone	Paraphernalia
Physicist	Pomegranate	Prevalent
Rateable	Receive	Release
Repartee	Scintillate	Transparent
Tweezer	Ultimatum	Vegetable
Vertebra	Wrath	Wrinkly

42 SWOT chart

Suggested applications
- Data analysis and problem-solving
- Encouraging creativity

What happens Participants work individually and then in small groups to explore an issue by identifying current and future strengths and weaknesses.

Purpose To help analyse and understand an organization's position and potential in a particular area.

Format Individual/small groups.

Resources A flipchart and marker pens.

Time 35–40 minutes, or as required.

Introductory notes A SWOT analysis is a method used by specialists and business planners to gain a strategic perspective on an issue or situation, and is a simple and valuable exercise for most skills or business meetings. It can be used to focus on one single set of skills or for an organization or group of individuals. Commonly used for marketing, a SWOT cart can just as easily be used to assess and project customer service, health and safety, cost management and recruitment issues, as well as many others.

When completing your example chart, where participants have good practices and skills, list these under 'Strengths'. In areas where hazards and risks exist, or you feel there is room for improvement, list these under 'Weaknesses'. The 'Opportunities' section is self-explanatory; it should list ideas which are not being fully developed and utilized. Threats constitute areas of concern and potential problems.

Procedure 1. Draw a SWOT chart on a flipchart page, listing in one column Strengths and the other column Weaknesses.

2. Complete the chart in terms of the issue at hand.
3. Distribute a copy of the handout to each participant and ask them to list their own perception of strengths, weaknesses, opportunities and threats with regard to themselves/a skill/their organization. Allow 10 minutes for this task.
4. Next, organize the participants into small groups and ask them to summarize their lists collectively on a flipchart page. Allow 20 minutes.
5. Review and discuss the charts one at a time.

Variations
- Give each group a focus for the SWOT chart – for example, their own personal skills, the company or organization's standing, marketing analysis or product review.
- After each group has displayed its chart, point out that sometimes opportunities can also simultaneously be threats. Furthermore, strengths and weaknesses are very often the same elements at different ends of the scale. Discuss any similarities and any differences between the groups' analyses.

SWOT chart

List strengths and weaknesses (or areas to improve), opportunities and threats (or areas of potential hazard) on the chart below.

Strengths	Weaknesses
Opportunities	Threats

43   Taking sides

Suggested applications
- Data analysis and problem-solving
- Planning improvements
- Energizer
- Encouraging creativity

What happens   Participants work with like-minded colleagues to develop their views and ideas on a particular issue, before reconvening and discussing further.

Purpose   To generate discussion and group interaction.

Format   Main group discussion.

Resources   Flipchart or a copy of the handout for each participant.

Time   25–30 minutes, or as required.

Procedure
1. Draw the diagram and instructions on a flipchart, or distribute a copy of the handout to each participant, **writing a controversial statement or point of view in the box first**.
2. Ask the participants to consider this statement and move to either the front of the room if they agree, the back if they disagree, or stay in the middle if they neither agree nor disagree.
3. Allocate the 'neutral' people to even the numbers of the 'fors' and 'againsts'.
4. Now give the two groups 10 minutes to discuss their views and prepare their arguments for and against the statement.
5. Chair a short debate between the two sides with participants contributing freely from each group. Allow 15 minutes or more for this, depending on the nature of the topic and meeting.
6. When the time is up, or agreement has been reached, discuss the issues arising and the approach taken by each side.

Note: This exercise encourages a black/white response, although many people think in 'shades of grey' on major issues – thereby avoiding making a choice or decision.

Be particularly alert for people who change their minds and try to disguise why they have changed their viewpoint, or people who have one opinion which is different from their own day-to-day behaviour. For example, a view that 'All smoking should be made illegal' may actually be supported by somebody who smokes.

Variation   By shortening the discussion time you can run this exercise several times with different controversial statements or viewpoints.

Taking sides

- Consider the statement below carefully.
- Decide if you are FOR or AGAINST and move to the FRONT or BACK of the room. If you have no particular view either way, stay in the MIDDLE of the room.

What is your opinion?

44   Team talents

Suggested applications
- Ice-breaker
- Energizer
- Building rapport
- Encouraging creativity

What happens   Participants identify and label their colleagues' skills, qualities and attributes.

Purpose   To highlight or review skills within a team, department or group of people.

Format   Small groups/main group discussion.

Resources   A flipchart and multi-coloured marker pens.
Flipchart pages and multi-coloured marker pens for each small group.
A copy of the handout for each participant (optional).

Time   10–15 minutes, or as required.

Procedure
1. Distribute a copy of the handout to each participant or draw the text (and illustrations) on to a flipchart.
2. Explain that this activity will allow participants to get to know their colleagues better than they do now and also allow them to share with others and see how others judge their skills and attributes.
3. Organize the participants into small groups, or run as a main group discussion. Distribute flipchart pages and coloured pens if using small groups and ask them to draw and label their colleagues as per the example on the handout/flipchart. Ask them to use different coloured pens for different people. Allow 10–15 minutes.
4. If running as a main group discussion, draw the participants' suggestions on the main flipchart.

Variation   Allow time for people to upgrade their illustrations as they get to know and work with their colleagues.

Team talents

Task

- Write the names of the team at random on a flipchart page.
- Through discussion attribute qualities to each person and write against their name.

Example

Alice – serious
good with numbers

Gary – sense of humour

Bob – happy,
bold

Francis – leadership
skills

45 Telephone skills quiz

Suggested applications

- Energizer
- Testing learning
- Focusing individuals
- Planning improvements

What happens
Participants work individually to complete telephone quiz sheets. They then mark and review them in pairs, ending the exercise with specific action points for improvement.

Purpose
To test participants' knowledge and awareness of key telephone skills. It is also a useful way of testing and reinforcing points from previous meetings.

Format
Individual/pairs.

Resources
A copy of the handout for each participant.
A copy of the 'Answers' handout.
A flipchart and pens.

Time
20–45 minutes, or as required.

Procedure
1. Before running the activity, complete it yourself, marking, and allocating scores to, the 'ideal' or 'right' answers – these will vary according to individual or organizational stances. A set of suggested answers is included on page 176.
2. Organize the participants into pairs.
3. Distribute a copy of the handout (quiz sheet) to each participant and ask them to work individually through the questionnaire, carefully and thoughtfully answering each question. Allow 10–15 minutes.
4. When everybody has finished, ask the participants to swap papers with their partners and mark each other's as you read out the answers. Defer any discussion until you have completed reading out all the answers.

5. Read out the answers (see 'Answers' on page 176).
6. Next, ask the participants to return their question sheets and review their scores and responses with their partner. Then go around the group asking people to read out their scores and discuss any questions that participants are not sure of or are marked wrongly.
7. Hold a main group review, writing up the key points on a flipchart.
8. Conclude the activity by asking each participant to circle the three questions on which they scored the lowest, and at the bottom of the page write down three actions that they can take to improve these areas (one for each).

Telephone quiz

1. Describe how you would place a customer on hold using your normal telephone.

2. How would you transfer a call to another extension?

3. You answer your telephone only to discover that the caller wants to speak to someone in a completely different department. Do you:

   a) Tell them they have come through to the wrong extension and put them back to the switchboard?
   b) Try to connect them yourself?
   c) Pretend you've got a bad line and hang up?

4. What is the optimum number of rings in which to answer a call?

   a) One
   b) Three
   c) Five

5. During a call you need to get some information that would take you a couple of minutes to retrieve. Do you:

   a) Ask the customer to wait?
   b) Ask them to call back?
   c) Take their number and call them back?
   d) Something else?

6. In a national survey of telephone users, what do you think was the most hated telephone bad habit?

   a) putting people on hold
   b) telephone music
   c) being able to hear the person talking/eating/chewing/drinking whilst on hold

cont'd

Reproduced from *50 Ways to Liven Up Your Meetings*, Graham Roberts-Phelps, Gower, Aldershot

7. You have been trying to get through to a particular prospect for several days, always unsuccessfully. Suggest three ideas for being more effective:

   a)
   b)
   c)

8. What are the three things that you should state at the beginning of an incoming call?

   a)
   b)
   c)

9. What are the three things that you should state at the beginning of an outgoing call?

   a)
   b)
   c)

10. How do you demonstrate active listening on the telephone?

11. What are three things that you should have ready or prepared before every sales call?

    a)
    b)
    c)

Improvement action 1

Improvement action 2

Improvement action 3

Telephone quiz: answers

1. Offer a choice of options (for example, 'Would you mind holding or can I call you back?'); go back to them every 30 seconds.

2. Give them the name and number of the person to whom you are transferring them, and pass on any information regarding the nature or identity of the call to the recipient.

3. b) Try to connect them yourself.

4. b) Three

5. c) Take their number and call them back

6. Eating on the telephone, but all the others were close!

7. Answers might include: try a different time of day; talk to his assistant and find an exact time to call; try another contact; send a fax and ask them to call you.

8. Answers might include: friendly greeting; name and company; 'How may I help you?'.

9. Answers might include: friendly greeting; name and company; purpose of call.

10. Answers might include: ask probing questions; use 'aha', 'yes' 'I see…'; short confirming statements.

11. Answers might include: pen and paper; an objective; customer information; prepared questions and answers to likely questions.

46   The plane hijacker

Suggested applications
- Ice-breaker
- Energizer
- Encouraging creativity

What happens   Participants work in pairs to ask questions and guess the answer to this puzzle.

Purpose   To practise creative and lateral thinking.

Format   Pairs.

Resources   A copy of the handout for each pair.
An OHP (optional).

Time   20–25 minutes, or as required.

Procedure
1. Ask the participants to work in pairs on this exercise, which will test their lateral thinking ability and creativity.
2. Distribute a copy of the handout to each pair, read the story out aloud, or display it as an OHP slide.
3. Allow the participants 10–15 minutes to solve the puzzle. During this time, you might choose to provide short 'yes' or 'no' answers to participants' questions (see 'The clues' below), but take care not to lead them too quickly to the answer. Encourage the participants to explore all possible options, thinking as laterally and creatively as possible.
4. When the time is up, go around the group, asking the pairs to read out their answers or conclusion.
5. Tell them the correct answer (see 'The answer' below).

The clues

Q: Did the man change his mind during the flight?

A: No.

Q: So he had always intended to leap out of the plane on his own?

A: Yes.

Q: Did he carefully choose one parachute in preference to the other?

A: No.

Q: Did he ask for two parachutes in order to deceive the authorities?

A: Yes.

The answer The hijacker asked for two parachutes, to make the authorities think that he was going to take a hostage with him. They therefore gave him two good parachutes. Had he asked for only one, they would have given him a dud. By asking for two he eliminated that risk. Once he knew that he had two good parachutes, either would do for his escape.

Variation Ask the participants to work on this problem in small groups, in order to create more of a group interaction and team-building exercise.

The plane hijacker

A true story

A few years ago in the USA, a young man hijacked a passenger flight at gunpoint. He ordered the pilot to fly to a different airport and radioed his demands to the airport authorities.

In return for the safe release of the plane and hostages, he asked for $100,000 in a bag and two parachutes.

When the plane landed, he was given the bag and two parachutes. He then instructed the pilot to fly at a fairly low altitude towards their original destination. When they were over a deserted part of the country, he strapped on one of the parachutes and, clutching the bag of money, he leapt from the plane. The second parachute was not used. He was never found.

You have to answer one question:

Why did he ask for two parachutes if we assume that he only ever intended to use one?

Reproduced from *50 Ways to Liven Up Your Meetings*, Graham Roberts-Phelps, Gower, Aldershot

47 Tongue twisters

Suggested applications
- Ice-breaker
- Energizer
- Building rapport

What happens　　Participants work in pairs to practise tongue twisters.

Purpose　　To sharpen thinking and get participants working in groups.

Format　　Pairs.

Resources　　A flipchart or OHP.

Time　　10–15 minutes, or as required.

Introductory notes　　Sir Laurence Olivier used to recite tongue twisters before he went on stage to help him overcome his terrible stage fright. He claimed that doing this helped him to relax and become more 'mentally fluent'. Reciting tongue twisters seems to have the same effect on other people too. Try a few the next time your people need a change of pace and a few laughs!

Procedure
1. Prepare by writing several of the following tongue twisters on a flipchart or OHP.
2. Explain that everyone is going to recite several tongue twisters to help synchronize their brains with their tongues, perhaps referring to Sir Laurence Olivier as an example.
3. Ask the participants to find a partner – preferably someone who hasn't played this game with them before.
4. Say: 'Whoever has the larger feet [anything can be substituted] will be partner Number One. You will recite the first tongue twister, three times in a row, as quickly as you can. Are you ready? We'll take ten seconds. Start right now.'
5. Continue: 'Now, it's time to give your partner a chance to

recite the second tongue twister, three times in a row, as quickly as possible. Get ready, partners, get set, go! Now, for the last tongue twister. Both of you will recite the third Tongue Twister aloud as quickly as you can. Start right now!'

Tongue twisters

- Trip thy tongue these titillating twisters
- Double bubble gum bubbles double.
- You know New York. You need New York. You know you need unique New York.
- Sixty-six sick chicks.
- Strange strategic statistic.
- The twine to three tree twigs.
- Pre-shrunk shirts.
- Shy Sarah saw six Swiss wristwatches.
- The sixth sheikh's sixth sheep's sick.
- Truly rural.
- The seething sea ceaseth, and thus seething sea sufficeth us.
- A bloke's back brake block broke.
- Does this shop stock short socks with spots?
- Three grey geese in the green grass grazing; grey were the geese, and green was the grazing.
- Sinful Caesar sipped his snifter, seized his knees, and sneezed.

48   True or false?

Suggested applications
- Ice-breaker
- Energizer
- Building rapport

What happens   Participants take it in turns to guess which statements that someone makes about themselves are true and which are false.

Purpose   To change pace or act as a break between sessions and to build rapport. It is also a good introductory activity at the start of a meeting or event.

Format   Main group discussion.

Resources   None.

Time   10–15 minutes, or as required.

Procedure
1. Explain that the objective of this activity is find out more about each other.
2. Ask the participants to write down **three** revealing things about themselves as follows:

   - Two should be true and perhaps unusual or unknown by other people in the room
   - One should be false – a complete lie

   For example: 'I have been chased by an escaped bull, bungee jumped from 150 feet off a cliff and failed my driving test five times.'

3. Allow the participants 5 minutes to write down their statements.
4. After all the participants have completed the questions, regain the group's attention and go around the group,

asking each participant to read out their three statements and then ask one person – perhaps the person on their left – to guess which is the false statement.

5. Run a brief discussion, using the 'Discussion points' below.

Discussion points

- What surprises were revealed?
- Based on what you discovered during the activity, what insights do you now have about each other?

49   Whistling cracker

Suggested applications
- Ice-breaker
- Energizer
- Building rapport

What happens   Participants compete in teams to see who is the first to be able to whistle after eating two or more cream crackers.

Purpose   To build rapport at the beginning of a meeting.

Format   Small groups.

Resources   Two or more cream crackers or water biscuits for each participant.

Time   10–15 minutes, or as required.

Procedure
1. Divide the group into two equal teams.
2. Have the teams stand or sit in lines facing each other, and give each participant two (or more!) cream crackers or water biscuits.
3. On a given signal, the first player in each team starts to eat their crackers; as soon as their mouth is clear enough to whistle, the second player in the team can start to eat and so on.
4. The first team in which all the players have whistled wins the contest.

50   Word magic

Suggested applications
- Ice-breaker
- Energizer
- Encouraging creativity
- Encouraging group-working

What happens   Participants work in pairs or small groups to ask questions and guess the answer to this puzzle.

Purpose   To build rapport and to sharpen thinking.

Format   Pairs/small groups.

Resources   A copy of the handout for each participant.

Time   5–10 minutes, or as required.

Procedure
1. Distribute a copy of the handout to each participant and ask them to work together in pairs or groups of three.
2. Allow them 5 minutes to complete the task.
3. Find out who has the most words.

Answers   presented, dependant, dependent, defendant, deterrent, pretender, preferred, presenter.

Word magic

Find eight nine-letter words, in any direction. Letters may be used more than once.

T	N	A
P	E	D
R	F	S

Appendix

Inspirational quotations

Display an interesting or thought-provoking quotation on a flipchart as participants enter the meeting room.

Whatever you can do, or dream you can … begin it. For Boldness has Genius, Power and Magic in it. Begin it NOW!! (*Goethe*)

He worked by day
And toiled by night
He gave up play
And some delight.
Dry books he read
New things to learn,
And forged ahead
Success to earn.
He plodded on
With faith and pluck,
And when he won
They called it luck. (*Anon.*)

A generous man will prosper; he who refreshes others will himself be refreshed. (*Proverbs 11:25*)

Folks who never do any more than they get paid for, never get paid for any more than they do. (*Elbert Hubbard*)

People who say something can't be done are usually interrupted by those doing it! (*Anon.*)

People who would never think of committing suicide or ending their lives would think nothing of dribbling their lives away in useless minutes and hours every day. (*Thomas Carlyle*)

Five percent of the people think, ten percent of the people think they think; and the other eighty-five percent would rather die than think. (*Anon.*)

Opportunity is often missed because we are broadcasting when we should be tuning in. (*Anon.*)

If one advances confidently in the direction of his own dreams and endeavours to live the life which he has imagined, he will meet with a success unexpected in common hours. (*Henry David Thoreau*)

Life is a battle from the beginning to the end. One of the biggest battles you will ever have will be with yourself. (*Dr Norman Vincent Peale*)

Not everything that is faced can be changed, but nothing can be changed until it is faced. (*James Baldwin*)

Most people plan their vacations better than they plan their lives. (*Mary Kay Ash*)

Winners never quit. Quitters never win. (*Vince Lombardi*)

Don't forget until too late that the business of life is not business, but living. (*B.C. Forbes*)

It takes less effort to keep an old customer satisfied than to get a new customer interested. (*Anon.*)

Life has been given to us, therefore it doesn't owe us anything. (*Gerhard Gschwandtner*)

If you can't write your idea on the back of a business card, you don't have a clear idea. (*Anon.*)

Lack of activity destroys the good condition of every human being, while movement and methodical physical exercise save and preserve it. (*Plato*)

A mistake at least proves somebody stopped talking long enough to do something. (*Anon.*)

Talking is like playing the harp. There is as much in laying the hand on the strings to stop their vibrations as in twanging them to bring out their music. (*Oliver Wendell Holmes*)

Problems are nothing but wake-up calls for creativity. (*Anon.*)

The tougher you are on yourself, the easier life will be on you. (*Zig Ziglar*)

People who are lost in their lives tend to follow people who are lost in their theories. (*Roger Gentis*)

The only place where success comes before work is in the dictionary. (*Anon.*)

You can make more friends in two months by becoming really interested in other people than you can in two years by trying to get other people interested in you. (*Dale Carnegie*)

We act as though comfort and luxury were the chief requirements of life, when all that we need to make us really happy is something to be enthusiastic about. (*Anon.*)

Adversity is the diamond dust heaven polishes its jewels with! (*Robert Leighton*)

Don't cut your life into years, weeks or days, but cut your days into lives. Then celebrate each moment as one full life. (*Gerhard Gschwandtner*)

We become what we think about. If we don't think, we become nothing. (*Earl Nightingale*)

You must make your mark on this earth, and, if you have never done so, it is simply because you neglected to use the powers you have, or have neglected to develop them. (*John Henry Patterson*)

When your mind is tired, exercise your body: when your body is tired, exercise your mind. (*Anon.*)

Nothing in the world can take the place of persistence.
Talent will not: nothing is more common than unsuccessful men with talent.
Genius will not: unrewarded genius is almost a proverb.
Education will not: the world is full of educated derelicts.
Persistence and determination alone are omnipotent.
The slogan 'press on' has solved and always will solve the problems of the human race. (*President John Calvin Coolidge*)

The best time to complete your daily plan is the night before. That way you'll wake up motivated and you won't be floundering around for half a day just defining what you want to accomplish. (*Tom Hopkins*)

Do a disagreeable job today instead of tomorrow. You will save 24 hours of dreading to do it, while having 24 hours to savour the feeling that the job is behind you. (*Anon.*)

Worry is misuse of the imagination. (*Mary Crowley*)

If you would hit the mark, you must aim a little above it: every arrow that flies feels the attraction of earth. (*Henry W. Longfellow*)

Quality IS productivity. (*Federal Express management manual*)

Try not to become a man of success but rather try to become a man of value. (*Albert Einstein*)

Imagination is more important than knowledge. (*Albert Einstein*)

Courage is the first of human qualities because it is the quality which guarantees all the others. (*Winston Churchill*)

If we open a quarrel between the past and the present, we shall find that we have lost the future. (*Winston Churchill*)

The empires of the future are the empires of the mind. (*Winston Churchill*)

For a man to achieve all that is demanded of him he must regard himself as greater than he is. (*Goethe*)

Our life is what our thoughts make it. (*Marcus Aurelius*)

The desire of gold is not for gold. It is for the means of freedom and benefit. (*Ralph Waldo Emerson*)

When I was young I thought that money was the most important thing in life; now that I am old I know that it is. (*Oscar Wilde*)

The aim of education should be to teach us rather how to think, than what to think; rather to improve our minds, so as to enable us to think for ourselves, than to load the memory with the thoughts of other men. (*James Beattie*)

Do or don't do, there is no try. (*Anon.*)

It is a descending stream of pure activity which is the dynamic force of the universe. (*Kabbalah*)

Enthusiasm is the leaping-lightning little understood by the horse-power of the understanding. (*Ralph Waldo Emerson*)

Whether you believe you can, or whether you believe you can't – you're right! (*Henry Ford*)

Learning is a kind of natural food for the mind. (*Cicero*)

You cannot teach a man anything; you can only help him to find it within himself. (*Galileo*)

Each day is the scholar of yesterday. (*Publilius Syrus*)

Reading maketh a full man; confidence a ready man; and writing an exact man. (*Francis Bacon*)

Crafty men condemn studies, simple men admire them, and wise men use them. (*Francis Bacon*)

Some men grow mad by studying much to know, but who grows mad by studying good to grow? (*Benjamin Franklin*)

Seeing much, suffering much, and studying much, are the three pillars of learning. (*Benjamin Disraeli*)

The best education in the world is that got by struggling to get a living. (*Wendell Phillips*)

There are three schoolmasters for everybody that will employ them … the senses, intelligent companions, and books. (*Henry Ward Beecher*)

To know how to suggest is the great art of teaching. (*Henri Frederic Amiel*)

Reading and writing, arithmetic and grammar do not constitute education, any more than a knife, fork and spoon constitute a dinner. (*John Lubbock*)

Education is what survives when what has been learnt has been forgotten. (*F. Skinner*)

How much you know is less important than how fast you are learning. (*Anon.*)

Only the educated are free. (*Epictetus*)

Knowledge increases in proportion to its use, that is, the more we teach the more we learn. (*P. Blavatsky*)

Learning is weightless … treasure you always carry easily. (*Chinese Proverb*)

What we have to learn to do, we learn by doing. (*Aristotle*)

The most valuable result of all education is the ability to make yourself do the thing you have to do, when it ought to be done, whether you like it or not. (*Thomas Huxley*)

Never regard study as a duty but as an enviable opportunity to learn to know the liberating influence of beauty in the realm of the spirit for your own personal joy and to the profit of the community to which your later works belong. (*Albert Einstein*)

And still they gazed, and still the wonder grew, That one small head should carry all it knew. (*Oliver Goldsmith*)

He might have been a very clever man by nature, but he had laid so many books on his head that his brain could not move. (*Robert Hall*)

The important thing is not to stop questioning. (*Albert Einstein*)

Teachers open the door … you enter by yourself. (*Chinese Proverb*)

The process of scientific discovery is, in effect, a continual flight from wonder. (*Albert Einstein*)